WAS I EVER LUCKY

How I Won the Lottery Called Life

Barbara Kersey

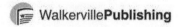

ISBN-13: 978-1466439177

ISBN-10: 1466439173

Was I Ever Lucky
by Barbara Kersey
edited by Elaine Weeks
© 2011 all rights reserved
published in Canada by Walkerville Publishing Inc.
716 Windermere Road Windsor ON N8Y 3E1
www.walkerville.com

printed in the USA

*First to my smart, caring, warm and
patient editor, Elaine Weeks.*

*To my children Grant, Sheila and Mark,
and their families.*

*To my American cousins Roderick Macdonald
and Christina and Brian Hunsberger.*

*To the Kersey-Brown-Holdsworth nieces and
nephews, great nieces and nephews, and great greats.*

*And to my dauntless and courageous friend,
Elsie Magowan.*

WHERE IT ALL STARTED

It's another perfect summer day in Essex County. The sky is a cloudless, brilliant blue. A soft breeze stirs the air.

I am sitting on the deck of Duffy's Tavern in Amherstburg, a short journey from the border city of Windsor, Ontario, with my good friend Doug Williamson Sr. We're enjoying some of their famous perch and the view across the water to BobLo Island. The two of us are quietly eating, savouring both the food and the moment, and lost in our own thoughts. When Doug suddenly asks a question, it literally seems to come out of the clear blue sky.

"How did you get here, Barbara?"

"I drove!" I reply thinking, is he kidding? Laughing, I remind him, "That's how we *both* got here."

But Doug doesn't laugh. I regard him closely, admiring his soft, curly silver hair, his rugged features – a handsome man. And he is definitely serious.

He explains, "Well, since I am a historian, I'd really like to know how your family got to Windsor from Nova Scotia."

Doug had been head of the History Department at Patterson Collegiate in the city. I recall him saying once how he fell in love with history as a boy.

I gaze at a passing freighter for a few moments to collect my thoughts. It's true. I also like knowing the answers to questions. In fact, I prick and probe where sometimes I shouldn't. I certainly remember the story of how my family got to Windsor even though I had been a little girl at the time; I have my own memories and the knowledge gleaned from pestering my mother.

"OK, if you must know Doug, I'll tell you how I got here."

After he moves his chair a little bit closer I begin.

"When I was about three, my mother took my little brother and I across the ocean on a ship. We sailed from Nova Scotia and went to my grandmother's home in Scotland. But it wasn't just a visit – we lived with her for about two years. Our father stayed back in Canada. My mother had told him she would return, but not to Nova Scotia. She said they must start anew."

"Hmmm," mutters Doug. I pause and look at him questioningly but he motions me to go on.

"My father was the oldest son so inherited the family farm in Gays River, Nova Scotia, and it had been waiting for him when he came back from WWI. My brother and I were the third generation of MacDonalds born there. But because of the troubles my parents were having, the farm, the cattle – everything was sold.

"Troubles? What kind of troubles?" asks Doug.

"Oh, I don't know – the usual troubles I suppose. Anyway, my father heard news about lots of jobs at Ford Canada in Windsor so he decided that was where we would start anew. I think it was 1923 when he arrived in Windsor; well, actually what was then the town of Walkerville, which as you know is next to Ford City. My mother, brother and I followed from Scotland two years later, just in time for me to start kindergarten.

My tale is done and I'm expecting some kind of response from Doug. He has turned to gaze at the freighter, which is slowly disappearing behind the island.

"And that's how I got here, Doug." I nudge him.

He remains quiet for a few moments and I'm wondering, what the heck is he thinking? He finally turns to me and says, "It must have been another woman."

Now where did this preposterous idea come from?

"What do you mean Doug?" I reply sharply.

"Those 'troubles'", Doug says, using his fingers as quotation marks. "That's what I'm talking about, Barbara." He crosses his arms and looks at me like I'm a bit dim.

After a moment or two to think this over, trying to imagine the unthinkable – my father with another woman – I exclaim, "Doug, this all happened a long time ago! You didn't even know my father. He was an absolute saint!"

"Barbara," he replies confidently, "it's always another woman."

I sit in stunned silence. Had my friend answered years of unasked questions? Suddenly a flood of memories comes rushing back and through the fog I begin seeing how Doug's words are making certain niggling incidents in my life make more sense.

I shake my head for if what he was saying were true my mother would have been unforgiving! And even if it were not it has definitely shaken me to the core. I wonder if my brother and I could possibly have been that naïve.

A few days later, I mention Doug's theory about our parents to my brother during a visit at his seniors' residence. As Ian has Alzheimer's he spends most of his time in the past; we frequently talk of those days.

At first he doesn't say a word but I notice his hands are clenching and unclenching the arms of his easy chair. I am worried I have upset him but he suddenly shakes his head like he's coming out of a trance and says, "I've often wondered what happened." He is quick to add, "He was a wonderful father and I loved him very much."

Well, me too. I thought the sun rose and set on him. He was the buffer that made life better. As children he would put us to bed, hear our prayers, then untuck the sheets to tickle our toes, sending us into gales of laughter.

Other bed times he would make funny shadow hand puppets on the wall, or maybe crank up the tall phonograph in the corner of the room to play a scratchy 78 rpm record of "Old MacDonald Had a Farm". My brother and I would happily moo and oink along with the music.

Yes, in my eyes he was still a wonderful father, but the lunch with Doug had definitely unsettled me. In fact, I felt like I had been struck by lightning. My thoughts about my past felt absolutely scrambled.

As I continued to process his theory for several weeks, I began to realize that even though events from my past were not what they seemed, this revelation was causing me to fully appreciate what a remarkable past it was.

I had long contemplated writing my family story but for one reason or another had put it off.

And then I turned 90. I knew it was now or never.

BEFORE MY TIME

Mary Theresa (Mollie) Burke was born in Helensburg, Scotland. Her birth certificate indicated that her father, Patrick Burke, was a Master Mason. The family was Catholic. Mollie was my mother.

Her father had come from the south of Ireland to work in the shipyards along the River Clyde, but died when she was just a baby, necessitating my grandmother taking her to live with relatives in Dumbarton. There they lived throughout my mother's school years.

My mother trained as a nurse in Carlisle. After she died, I found a certificate noting that she was trained to care for mental patients This training was very ironic, as you will see.

My father was born in Gays River, Nova Scotia, the eldest in a family of eight boys. Father was related to just about everyone in the community where everyone was a farmer.

He was already in the militia when war broke out in 1914 and he soon went overseas with the 17th Nova Scotia Highlanders. After training at Val Cartier, the regiment camped on Salisbury plain and that is where my parents met. My mother was working as a nurse in a nearby hospital. My father served for four years in the trenches along the Somme, with trips to the field hospital in Boulogne for gunshot and shrapnel wounds. Early on they met and fell in love and married in Hythe, England in 1915.

My mother came to Halifax in 1918 and stayed with my grandparents. These were happy times; she spoke of the Prince of Wale's visit, selling tags for the new Grace Hospital, going to tea dances.

My father travelled to Buckingham Palace to receive the Military Cross from King George V for bravery in action. Afterwards, he was kept for a year overseas for general demobilization.

By the time the two met up again Halifax they were not the same people who had married during the war.

And then there was the move to the farm. After Ian and I were born something happened that my astute friend Doug alluded to many years later, although I'm still not sure what it was.

Whatever this problem was, my father had to give up the farm and sell everything if he wanted his family back.

The brothers were all born on the farm at Gays River, N.S. My father was the eldest; the youngest by 19 years was his brother Clyde. Only three of the boys in his family lived to adulthood, and only one lived to old age.

Twice, two boys in the MacDonald family died on the same day from one of the terrible diseases rampant at that time. My grandfather's unmarried sister, Aunt Mary Anne (not an agreeable person from all accounts) never moved away from the farm. One day she walked up the hill to the house of her cousin Peter MacDonald, where there were children stricken with diphtheria. She noticed the children had runny noses and took out her hankie to wipe them. She returned to my grandparents and wiped their two sons' noses with the same hankie. Two boys died in short order and people told me of the little caskets displayed in the window. No one could enter the houses. Her cousin's two children later died from another outbreak of a different disease.

The boy who would have been my Uncle Ernest had a tragic ending. When I heard the story it made me cry. He was a student at Carroll's Corner one-room schoolhouse in Gays River, when another pupil pulled his chair out from under him. He fell in such a manner as to injure his back and died a short time later of meningitis.

Life was indeed harsh. At the time of the Halifax Explosion in 1917 my grandmother Christiana MacDonald was on the landing half way up the staircase of their Halifax home helping the girl hang clean curtains. She was found at the end of the yard and was never in good health again. But her spirit was strong and she told the doctors she would live to see her boys home from war, and she did. And a few years later, she saw and held me, the first girl born in the family in a very long time.

My father's cousin, Pearl Wiles, compiled stories her own mother told her of her youth as a girl in Gays River. She was Katherine McKeen and her parents were my great grandparents. Their farm home was named Willow Lane for the drive lined with willow trees, leading to the house. The trees are long gone.

Katie was born in 1867. Her father was William McKeen, my great grandfather. D. G. Macdonald was my grandfather.

When she was five Katie started attending the school at Carroll's Corner. Her first teacher was her sister Margaret. They would take a farm wagon to school, then fasten a note to the wagon and the horse, Nell, would find her own way back to Willow Lane. I suppose the note was in case the horse took to wandering.

After school Katie had to help with the work around the house. One of her most detested jobs was making candles. Every fall they would make a whole year's supply of them. They were made chiefly of mutton fat poured into moulds.

Every summer, after the sheep shearing, the wool had to be picked over before going to the mill to be carded. There were two spinning wheels at Willow Lane and it was the job of the women of the house to spin the yarn. Then came the all-important task of knitting stockings, mitts, socks, etc. from the yarn.

During the long winter months everyone knitted. Grandmother McKeen was an expert knitter and would often sit in the dark in the evenings, busy with her needles. The men's clothes were always made of natural coloured wool, but the feminine articles usually had a bright strip of red around the edge.

The most tedious job was that of weaving the yarn into cloth for dresses, blankets, etc. Each daughter got several blankets for her wedding gift. Occasionally a tailor would be called in to make suits or pants for the men. Her father used to make trips to Halifax to sell produce and he would bring home a web of unbleached cotton to be made into sheets, aprons and pillowcases.

Practically all the toys were home made. Her brother, Gordon made sleds from which they used to coast down a little hill near the back of the house. Her father made wooden dolls. One of her most prized possessions was a large rag doll made by her sister Christiana (my grandmother). She called it Selena Theakstone after a friend of the family.

Katie made her first visit to Halifax when she was about 14 years old. Her father and D. G. Macdonald took her with them in the wagon. It was a big event in her life. They started early in the morning and by nightfall arrived at Mr. Marshall's place near Waverly where they spent the night and early the next morning they continued on their journey to Halifax. (I think Gays River is about 28 miles from Halifax).

In around 1891 Katie left the farm for Truro where she was employed as a companion to an aged lady, Mrs. Fleming, who paid her $100 a year.

Life for my family in those days was certainly difficult and dangerous. Going back further in time, I discovered my great great great great ancestor, John McKeen and his wife died on the same day – December 30,

1767. I was told it was from some kind of flu. They lie in the Truro Cemetery and apparently they once lay next to the church (which is where they placed important Presbyterians when they died) but the church is long gone. Their tombstones are identical except for first names and age. A graceful F stands in for the letter S. His stone reads:

HERE LYES BURIED
THE BODY OF
JOHN McKEEN Efq
WHO DEPARTED THIS
LIFE, DECEMBER 30, 1767
AGED 67 Years
THE RIGHTEOUS FHALL BE HELD IN
EVERLAFTING REMEMBRANCE

I am proud of my Nova Scotia roots but how different and challenging my life would have been if we had not moved to Windsor. I can certainly say *"Was I ever lucky."*

FIRST MEMORIES

I am sitting on a faded chintz couch with my little brother Ian. We are at my Great Aunt Katie Wiles's home in Truro, Nova Scotia. I am about three. The two of us are playing with peg clothespins, which have spilled from a cloth bag.

Our mother is about to take us on a ship. We are heading for Scotland where we are to live with her mother. On the voyage I am deathly ill from seasickness. A steward runs in and out of the cabin, trying to help.

During the two years with my Grandmother Burke at her cottage by Loch Lomond I remember just two things distinctly: the lovely rocking horse in her garden, which I rode as often as I was allowed, and visiting a house with a very dark room with someone in a high bed. There was the most horrible stench. I suppose it was some relative or a close friend who was dying or we wouldn't have been there.

And then I dimly remember a long boat trip back to Canada to a new life.

ARRIVING IN WINDSOR: HOW SOCIAL NETWORKING WORKED IN THE 1920S

It wasn't the country club, the Women's Economic Forum, the Rotary Club or the Internet. In the 1920s, our connection to society and the community in Windsor was the church.

When my father arrived in town he knew no one. His first step was to look around for somewhere home-like to stay. By some miracle he chose to have room and board with the George Carter family on Gladstone near Wyandotte. We were all to become lifelong friends.

On his first Sunday in Windsor, the Carters invited my father to their church, which was Methodist. He politely declined and walked over to the corner of Windermere and Niagara to First Presbyterian where he got the shock of his life.

The last time he had seen the minister, the Rev. Dr. Melvin, was at the home of his McKeen grandparents in Nova Scotia. My father was soon installed as an elder and began teaching a Sunday school class of older boys.

For the MacDonald family the die was set.

Dr. James Young was another church elder. He occupied a house on Devonshire just north of Wyandotte that also served as his office. He became our general practitioner. The common bond between Dr. Young and my father, in addition to being Presbyterian, was books. Both men were avid readers.

Another elder was Fred Westover who owned the nearby drug store, which stood on the southwest corner of Ottawa Street at Hall Avenue. My father went to him for advice on where to find a good dentist and an eye doctor.

Fred knew a pretty good dentist, but the only thing was once in a while he took off on a toot and was two or three days getting over it. Otherwise, he was fine. As he lived near the church and was not a quiet drinker, we knew in advance when he would not be in his office.

As for eye doctors, Fred mentioned a young man just setting up practice across the street whose name was Boley and was married to a family doctor.

My father crossed the street and climbed the stairs to the second storey to speak to the small, neat young man who would become our eye doctor right until he ended his practice, at the ripe old age of 90.

Over the years, Dr. Boley became a known eccentric and at times sorely tried our patience. He turned up at family funerals, including my husband's, many years later. He repositioned me and my children near the casket and then announced, "I like that casket. I think I'll go downstairs and see about getting the same for myself." The four of us looked at each other and shrugged, once again accepting our doctor's odd behaviour.

Dr. Boley had no sense of time and you had to be prepared to wait. For him, appointment times meant nothing. One day my mother was waiting in his office on Ouellette Avenue for drops in her eye for Glaucoma. She had been sitting in the waiting room for quite some time when she heard furniture being moved and the doctor's voice directing his nurse to push and shove.

My mother could be fearsome and was up in a flash to knock on his door and call him out. His tiny frame appeared in the doorway and he had a startled look on his face.

"I do not mind sitting here all day for you to see your patients," my mother said, glaring at him, "but I refuse to wait another minute while you move furniture."

The tired patients in the waiting room applauded her audacity for this was not a time when you talked back to the doctor.

For many years, Dr. Boley would call me at home to talk. When he reached 90 years of age, he called to tell me that he was not as swift as he had been. Doctors in either London or Toronto had done a procedure, which discovered that he had moisture on the brain. They would have to operate.

"Don't do it," I said, although I had no basis of any kind for that advice. He went ahead and had it done and never practiced again.

There was something comforting about doctors in those days. Dr. Boley would say things like, "I remember your father," or, "I remember when Ian was taken prisoner of war," and when I got glaucoma, "I remember your mother had it." You weren't a faceless body in a crowded waiting room, even if you did have to wait an eternity.

FITTING IN

Shortly after my brother, mother and I arrived in Windsor my father joined the Old Country Club at St. Andrew's Presbyterian Church in downtown Windsor as he thought that would please my mother.

The Club consisted entirely of Scots and they met regularly in each other's homes. No liquor was ever served, just tea and biscuits, but nevertheless it was a lively group. Everyone always gathered around the piano to lustily belt out the old Scottish ballads. They all carried a small book of Scottish songs: "Scots Wa Hae," "Bonnets off Bonnie Dundee", and "Annie Laurie" were favourites, though sometimes they ventured into "Men of Harlech" despite it being a Welsh song. I had a copy of the book all these years until fairly recently when someone borrowed it and sad to say, never returned it.

I was sent to piano lessons but any dreams my father had of me playing for the Old Country Club were soon dispelled. I was by no means a success at piano playing.

The evenings always ended the same way, with the group around the piano singing "Auld Lang Syne" or perhaps it was "Will Ye Noo come Back Again" or maybe "God Be with you 'Till We Meet Again."

After writing this, passage I went to bed dreaming of kilted warriors. I realize those few years – the gap between WWI, which ended in 1918 and the Great Depression, which began in 1929 only to end with another world war in 1939 – were the most peaceful of my generation.

When my father inherited the MacDonald farm, his two remaining brothers, Clyde and Frank, received money their parents had put away in an effort to make things more equal. Frank and his wife Alice (he had married a Miss Locke from Lockeport) moved to Dartmouth. He held a senior position with Maritime Telephone and Telegraph and upon his retirement he was asked to take over a Bell Museum but he chose not to move and took up painting instead.

Meanwhile, Clyde followed my father to Windsor, and then moved to Detroit to attend the Ford Motor Co. Tool and Die School. The brothers were close and Clyde was at our home often. When the Depression hit he, along with two or three friends, left home to look for work. His journey led him to an Indiana farm where he married the farmer's daughter and that is how I have American cousins. Like all the MacDonalds, Clyde was handsome and had a good sense of humour. And sadly, like my father, he too had a major stroke in his 50s.

OUR NEIGHBOUR BULL, THE BOOTLEGGER

Our first home in Windsor was just outside distiller Hiram Walker's company town of Walkerville in a small house on Moy Avenue between Giles Boulevard and what was then Huron Street (later Richmond). This was during the second half of the 1920s. Eventually, we moved a few blocks east to Lincoln Road in Walkerville and our eastern progression continued: we moved to Windermere the next street east, and finally to Chilver, one more street east.

Prohibition was in full force when we lived on Moy. This was the period in history in which the manufacture, sale and transportation of intoxicating liquors was outlawed. In Michigan, it lasted from 1919 until 1933 while in Ontario it ran from 1917 to 1930.

In Windsor, where alcohol continued to be made for export just one mile away from Detroit, some Windsorites made fortunes "rum-running" on the Detroit River.

Across the alley and down a bit from our house was the home of the Bull Fielding family. Bull had an enormous garage at the back of the property, which was rumoured to be full of liquor and he was said to be a big time bootlegger.

Bull was a big man in size and reputation. The few times I saw him he never smiled.

Often at night our family was awakened by the sound of gunfire and then police sirens, followed by frantic activity in the alley.

Sure enough, Bull's men were returning from a run to the border where they had made a liquor delivery with the police in hot pursuit.

Working for Bull was certainly a hazardous occupation.

And for the MacDonald family, it was all mind-boggling and a far cry from our quiet Nova Scotia farm.

BEFORE WONDER DRUGS

When I was five and newly arrived in Windsor, the Board of Health, or its equivalent, started a program to immunize children with a general vaccination. This was in 1925 and seemingly this program, which took place in the schools, had never occurred before.

Students were lined up – class by class, and a doctor pricked each child in the arm.

The same needle was used on every girl and boy.

There were about five of us at Prince Edward School who almost immediately became seriously ill. They intended to hospitalize me (as the others had been) but I screamed so much I was allowed home with a doctor coming every morning to care for me.

At first, Dr. Trimble, a very nice young doctor near the school was called but as he was already ill himself with TB, he didn't have the stomach or strength to deal with such a seriously ill child. Dr. Brockenshire, who had an office near our house at Parent and Erie Street, was called next and declared he was up for the task.

He made a big slash on the back of my upper left arm and did what had to be done. Afterwards, every morning for months, Dr. Brockenshire would arrive with his black bag, take my temperature, and then kneel down beside me at the edge of the bed. He would take out his tweezers and begin pulling and pulling a great length of what looked like dressing for a wound from the large opening in the back of my arm and then repack the opening with new gauze.

The chairman of the Board of Education would come by the house frequently, promising to cover all medical costs. When I finally recovered, I had missed school for a whole year so was older than my peers.

Soon after my ordeal, a law was passed and each vaccination required a new needle. Dr. Brockenshire left family practice shortly after this incident to become an orthopaedic surgeon. In later years people said he was brilliant but gruff.

He was never gruff with me. *I was very lucky to have had him.*

"ROTHESAY VACATION" HOLIDAYING IN AMHERSTBURG

In the 1920s, British comedians made jokes about people vacationing at Blackpool. I have never been, but I assume that was where the "common folk" went.

My mother talked lovingly of vacationing at Rothesay, a resort on the west cost of Scotland. It is easily accessible from Glasgow, mostly by steamers on the River Clyde. Again, I was never there.

Our vacations were much closer by. Just before the Depression, my father had become friendly with Mr. Anger who owned a farm almost in the city and a couple of doors from what is now Highway 18. Dad broached the possibility of the Angers taking us in as summer guests. Mr. Anger talked it over with his wife and she was agreeable.

And that is how our family travelled to Amherstburg for a holiday. My father accompanied us to the depot near downtown Windsor and put my mother, Ian and me on the streetcar; we were met at the other end by a member of the Anger family.

Were we ever lucky!

The Detroit River was literally at their doorstep and as this was before the channel was dug through the river we were perfectly safe swimming in it. Each afternoon my mother gathered up towels, and the two of us, and we joined other families for a swim.

We were free to roam the property and surrounding area, which was relatively safe as the number of people owning cars being minimal. We sat down three times a day to the most scrumptious farm meals, served home style in big serving bowls. We enjoyed room and board for two weeks with my father joining us for the weekends. Ian and I made lots of friends who came to the streetcar stop to wave us goodbye when it was time to return to Windsor.

OUR DISNEY WORLD: BOBLO ISLAND

BobLo Island is a small oasis in the Detroit River lying about 18 miles south and west of Windsor, opposite the town of Amherstburg, Ontario. When approaching it in the 1920s on one of the two steamers that ran regularly all summer from downtown Detroit and Amherstburg, one saw a green paradise. If it wasn't your first trip, you knew that under the lush leafy trees lay a world of wonder...our Disney World.

There were dizzying rides, a huge dance hall, a sandy beach, a small golf course, ample picnic areas and places for groups to hold their own games – simply everything one could ask for.

In those days, July 1 was the greatest day of the year. Hundreds of families carrying their big picnic baskets would stream to the riverfront to board the boat for BobLo. Everyone was dressed in good clothes. I can still see my father in shirt, tie, straw boater and my mother wearing a lovely hat.

When we at last stepped onto that magical island, the children – hearts bursting with excitement, would dash ahead to pick out a picnic table and help clear it of the annual fish fly infestation.

Mother and father would follow with the picnic basket, which was always covered with a neatly folded tablecloth. They would shake out the cloth and spread it over the chosen table. Mother had packed her everyday china and cutlery and her own teapot, as all the mothers did; boiling water was provided. We were to feast on freshly made potato salad, egg sandwiches, peanut butter and jam sandwiches, and cold meat sandwiches all made with fresh bread, and for dessert: butter tarts, or perhaps cupcakes.

But the food was of secondary interest to us children. We were chafing at the bit to go play. First we were literally off to the races: 3-legged, egg on a teaspoon, and others, followed by a go at some of the rides. As a child my very favourite ride was the Whip but when I entered my teens it was the dance pavilion that was the main attraction for me. Big bands played and I think the cost was 10 cents a dance.

We would always make our way to the bathing beach to cool off. I cherish the picture of my father on the shore of the beach, pant legs rolled up, straw boater on, romping with us.

For several summers, the three local churches in our hometown of Walkerville, Ontario – St. Mary's Anglican, Chalmers United and Lincoln Road United, joined together for the July 1 venture.

Sunday school teachers and pupils received free tickets for the boat. Our minister, the Rev. Mr. Morden always hurried down the gangplank as soon as we landed, carrying his golf clubs and then would promptly disappear. To this day I can't recall ever seeing that golf course.

One year, we were barely back in the house from our trip when my brother Ian started to swell up in enormous bumps. My father took one look and pronounced, "poison ivy."

My mother, newly arrived from Scotland, had never heard of or seen such a thing and went crazy as Ian jumped up and down, ran in circles and screamed in pain. She phoned Dr. Guest, who went to our church and lived nearby at the corner of Lincoln Road and Richmond Street. He looked at Ian and he too pronounced, "poison ivy."

My father handed over $5 and then proceeded to mix up a large amount of a special solution the doctor recommended, which was to be applied several times a day until Ian was well.

And then Ian began to shed his skin, all over the house.

It turned out he and some friends had wandered into some poison ivy infested bushes near the dance pavilion. Despite this unpleasant experience no one was deterred from attending next year's picnic.

There is nothing I know today that compares to the excitement and fun of those July the firsts.

A FAMOUS EVANGELIST VISITS WINDSOR

In the 1920s there was a renowned team of Canadian evangelists, Crossley and Hunter, who had made a big mark both in Canada and in the U.S. One day the Rev. Hunter, a son of the evangelist, came to speak in the Chapel in the Woods at the Jack Miner bird sanctuary in Kingsville. Not only was he a cousin to Miss Hunter who taught music at Prince Edward School, he was related to the Davidson family of our church, so off drove a few carloads of our congregation to hear him speak.

I was mesmerized by the whole affair and hung on to his every word. And then he raised his arm and pointed behind us. I turned and saw a path leading into the darkness of dense foliage. At that moment, Mr. Hunter's voice boomed out, "I heard a voice behind me say, this is the way! Walk thou in it."

I nearly died of a heart attack. My body shook. I half expected the Lord God himself to appear.

I was 14 years old and I still remember this as though it happened yesterday.

ABOVE AND BEYOND

One day in the mid 1920s, I asked my mother, "Where does Daddy and Mr. Cook, (a neighbour) go in their best suits on Sundays before church?"

She told me not to tell anyone but they went to the jail and held church service for inmates.

"THE JAIL!" I was shocked and believe me I didn't tell anyone for it didn't sound too savoury to me.

Now I know these men were ahead of their time.
I never asked my father about this.

A MATTER OF CONSCIENCE

On Sundays we ate diner at noon, after church. Inevitably, it was roast beef, mashed potatoes, and a vegetable or two. Beef was 15 cents a pound at the market and a family got several meals out of a roast —perhaps shepherd's pie the next day or a stew. I doubt that anyone had heard of a casserole.

One day the minister asked the Elders and board of management to stay after church. We waited and waited at home for my father to arrive so that we could eat.

When he finally showed up we asked about the meeting and he explained that Mr. Lowe, who built the home often referred to as the Paul Martin House on the corner of Devonshire and Ontario, had offered to pay for the painting of the church, which was sorely needed. At issue was whether they could, as Presbyterians, accept money earned from the sale of liquor.

There was a long and heated debate before they finally accepted since the Lowe son attended Sunday School, as did the son from the Cooper family of Cooper Court, another enormous home (demolished years later) built by a rumrunner kitty corner to Mr. Lowe's house. One of those two boys wore a coonskin coat to church, the first I had seen outside of pictures of crooner Rudy Vallee.

HAPPY ENDING

Over the years First Presbyterian became Chalmers United, with a big congregation and an extremely active Young People's group. Art Mingay, who later became President of Canada Trust, was the president and I was the secretary and that group had wonderful times. I spent a lot of it laughing.

We were busy at and around the church and enjoyed scavenger hunts in the neighbourhood and square dances in the church hall.

About a dozen years ago the Chalmers closed. If I were to look back and ask why, I'd say the search committees did not pick the right clergy. We even had new ministers coming in with their own agenda. WHAT NERVE.

In the old days, on Communion Sunday, the elders solemnly marched into the church and took the front seats. There were about 24 of them, all men, all white. Communion Sunday was special and those men with formal morning attire wore it. In my mind, I can still see them: Dr. Young, Dr. Deans and Roderick Campbell.

Fast forward to Spring 2010. At a Communion service at my current church, Riverside United, three black women, four white women and four white men served communion, again reflecting the good changes not only in the church but in our country.

Even more noteworthy is the fact that the once white bastion called Chalmers United is now home to a black congregation from Detroit.

Is that God at work or what?

DESPERATE DAYS:
The Depression as seen through the eyes of a little girl

Home economics had just started at school. One wonderful day we set out plain crackers, put a thin piece of cheese on each one and popped a whole tray of them in the oven. Heavenly.

I raced home to tell my family of this wonder. But, it seemed the very next day, all "frills" were taken from the school curriculum.

A short time earlier, my father's uncle in New Glasgow died and left him some money. There was much discussion as to what to do with it. My father finally took someone's advice and bought a chunk of land on University Avenue near Askin Boulevard for it was predicted that the city would grow quickly westwards.

And then – wham! The stock market crashed in 1929. In just days everything was lost – the land, our house, and our sense of security.

It was the beginning of the Great Depression.

That Christmas, our house, which would normally be awash with presents from Nova Scotia, was much different. My father was from a large extended family but strangely many did not marry and we were the only children. We were dear to our cousins and I suppose we reciprocated.

One day I heard my mother telling my father that she was writing to the relatives to tell them stop sending Christmas presents. No doubt she would be abrupt in her Scottish manner and she would not tell them we were in financial difficulty.

That first Christmas without presents Ian and I got cheap woollen gloves with a quarter in one thumb. Fortunately Great Aunt Minnie McGregor paid no attention to my mother and sent us each a classic book – "Hans Brinker" for Ian and "Little Women" for me. A bachelor friend of the family stopped by and gave Ian and I each a dollar bill and Grannie Burke in Scotland, (as she always did until she died) sent us each a pound note, which was worth $5- that was quite a sum in those days.

But despite these gifts, my little brother Ian who must have been about seven that year, wandered around asking, "Where are the presents?" I was sad for him as he looked for a dump truck, a toy automobile, a board game. But for the first time, I felt a great strength stirring in me. I said nothing to make things worse. I was all of nine years old.

Fathers did what they could to make money but it seemed that even if small jobs popped up, they somehow still had leisure. My father had a big vegetable garden as behooves a farmer. He sent to places in the west coast of the U.S. for seeds. When he produced tiny tomatoes, both red and yellow varieties, the neighbours predicted they would never catch on. But they did – about 60 years later.

My father also set himself up in the basement at a homemade desk and wrote poetry. And he had an easel at which he sketched animated characters. He showed us that if you flipped the pages, they produced a moving image. He explained to us that he was cartooning and that was how it was done in Hollywood. Cartoons were big at the movies and five cents got you into the school auditorium on Friday nights for a Charlie Chaplin film and a cartoon.

A few years later when I was in Grade 8 one of my classmates came over to ask me to the movies. He had a whole lot of friends following him. It sure was a surprise to me. I hadn't yet thought of boys, let alone dating. My mother answered the door and the boy asked if he could take me to a movie, but she told him no.

When I asked my mother why she said that to him she replied, "If it was a matter of us paying, we don't have the money."

Frequently men came by and asked if the lady of the house had any gold jewellery for sale. My mother often took them up on their offer, handing over lovely brooches and rings for a pittance I suppose.

Down the block Mr. Sanders had a barber chair set up in his kitchen and cut hair for 25 cents. Behind our house Mr. Gibbs built a horseshoe pitch in his back yard and it became a popular place. Another neighbour gave hair permanents to ladies in her kitchen and another candled eggs, putting aside the cracked, which she sold cheaply.

Some children still got new shoes but their parents went to the shoemaker to have theirs repaired. In the left hand corner of the top drawer of his tall dresser, my father kept a pair of lovely brown leather gloves. When

I asked about them he said, "Those were the gloves I wore when I shook hands with King George V and received the Military Cross."

One very cold day I noticed him wearing them; there was probably no money for a new pair. In most cases the children did not do without. We would have had warm gloves while the parents had the worries and the deprivation.

Towards the end of the Depression, my father began working as an inspector with the Department of Agriculture but he died before completing a month's work. The area head came to our house, full of apologies, to present my mother with a registered letter from the Federal Government ordering her to give back his salary. There was no pension or any support and even I knew this latest blow was wrong.

But it was all not doom and gloom. My growing up years in the 1920s and 1930s were in fact quite charmed. I swam off George Avenue when the Detroit River was relatively clean. My neighbours and I attended every baseball game The Hornets (of the Walkerville Baptist Church) played.

I rode the streetcars to downtown Windsor and for five cents crossed on the ferries to and from Detroit where I could safely walk up Woodward to the Masonic Auditorium. The Ford Sunday Evening Hour concerts – featuring the best of the best – were free. A wonderful Sunday evening cost almost nothing. Or, I watch the big bands play in downtown Detroit hotels or on stage at various movie houses.

There were vacant lots in most blocks and neighbourhood fathers flooded them in winter for skating. If we were feeling adventurous, my friends and I would walk to Windsor's Wigle Park on Erie Street, which was kept flooded all winter. There was a changing hut with a pot-bellied stove, which an attendant kept going. We would leave our overboots there with no fear that someone would swipe them. This was all free.

Ten cents got us into one theatre or another every Saturday to see wonderful movies or great musicals. We walked home discussing them, or, carefree, singing the songs from the show, like, "I won't dance, don't ask me."

For many of my growing up years, we lived next door to the Beckerson family. They had two girls, Shirley and Arletta, and we were immediately fast friends. In the summers they packed a couple of tents and took me along up north to camp on Wasaga Beach for two weeks.

It was absolute heaven. All these years later I still talk to Arletta. She married Bob Mephan who became Colonel of the Windsor Regiment – Tank Division. (My own brother became Lt. Col. of the Windsor Regiment – Tank, and then of the Essex Scottish. I don't know of anyone else achieving that.)

A few years later, I became inseparable from the two oldest girls of the Fred Stevens family: Elizabeth and Pat. That family also began to include me in outings and for many summers I was in the car with them as they headed to Mary Lake in Muskoka for two weeks.

What a marvellous time that was. The stars in the night sky seemed close enough to touch and the walk back along the country road from a movie in Huntsville never worried their parents.

Some days Mrs. Stevens packed a lunch for us, and Pat and I went off in the canoe to a neighbouring island to swim and sun and dream.

I even made myself useful by putting worms on the hook when Mr. Stevens went fishing, as his girls were too afraid to touch them. Often we had fresh fish for breakfast.

Elizabeth married Bud Wild who became head of the journalism department at University of Western Ontario, as well as a lifelong friend.

Looking back, the hard times were thankfully tempered by the kindness of others.

Was I ever lucky.

TEEN YEARS

Like most of the girls my age, I joined the Girl Guides and went to meetings at the old Walkerville post office where Don Gordon's sister Millie was our Guide captain. Their family ran the License Bureau. The Guide camp was on the waterfront in Puce a small community east of Windsor and I slogged around town selling Girl Guide cookies until I had sold enough to pay my way.

I was also attending C.G.I.T. (Canadian Girls in Training) at church. One day I told my father I didn't want to go to Sunday school any more, or CGIT or any of the other things. He said, "Fine, but you must have a church affiliation."

So I joined my church's Young People's group and fell in love with everyone. I was right where I should be. As it was such a well-attended group the United churches had an overall body and I ended up on the executive. It's full name was the Border Cities Young People's association, or BCYPU. We met and planned joint events. Huge fun.

I stood first in the class at school so my father arranged for me to go to Y Camp Robin Hood on Pelee Island. It was a wonderful experience and I knew I was extremely lucky to have gone.

In those days we saw every big movie at the Capitol Theatre in downtown Windsor on Saturday afternoons for 10 cents. Saturday evenings we paid 25 cents for an evening's dancing at the Y. We walked to the event and home and were perfectly safe on our city streets.

A major highlight for me during my teen years was attending the Military Ball at Walkerville Collegiate. My friend and neighbour, Jean Maitland, had an aunt known to me as Mrs. Jensen who lived on Chilver facing the park. She made Jean's dress and then offered to make mine. I didn't know what I'd do otherwise so this was a fabulous offer. The material and findings came to $11 and Mrs. Jensen charged $5 to make it.

The dress was a heavenly sky blue with a sweetheart neckline and a full skirt and when I put it on my mother smiled with pleasure. A smile from my mother was such a rare event that I've never forgotten that moment.

MEETING THE GREAT PAUL ROBESON

During the 1920s and 1930s there was a very famous African-American activist and singer named Paul Robeson. He had taken every award possible at Rutgers University, became a lawyer but was then turned out of his New York firm due to anti-black sentiment. This unfortunate event would prove to be fortuitous.

He turned to singing and acting where once again, he shone. Jerome Kern and Oscar Hammerstein wrote the song "Ol' Man River" for him and it became his signature. His rich baritone and his acting skills became known all over he world.

Robeson wanted to do more for his fellow African-Americans and became enamoured with Communism and the U.S.S.R. He traveled there several times. The American government subsequently cancelled his passport and, for a while, he was persona non grata in the U.S.

Who would have thought that I would be lucky enough to run into this magnificent man in Windsor, Ontario?

In approximately 1938, there was a prominent family living in the west end of Windsor by the name of Rodd. The father was part of a prestigious law firm, though what was unusual for the times, it wasn't the husband we read about in the papers, it was his wife.

At that time the west end had some really lovely homes (and still does though not as many) and the Rodds lived in one. Through some sort of connection my mother became friendly with an activist, Mrs. Leader, who lived on Indian Road on that side of town. Even though I was a shy teenage girl, Mrs. Leader must have noticed how I absorbed everything that came my way; she was intent on opening doors for me.

At this time Canada and particularly the U.S., were afraid of Russia and what Communism represented. Communists were known as "Reds". Apparently Mrs. Rodd was a sympathizer and referred to in the papers as "pink." Some people were nervous to be seen with her.

Returning from one of her trips to Russia, Mrs. Rodd asked Mrs. Leader and some friends to her home. Mrs. Leader asked me to come along. I knew it would be a political message though I was uninformed as to the meeting's true intent. Undeterred, I hopped a bus and when I arrived at the big west end home everything was in darkness. I could not see a light on anywhere and wondered if I had been given the wrong address.

I knocked and was admitted into total darkness with a "shush" so I would keep quiet. My eyes were slowly able to make out shapes when, from the dusk of the living room, a huge man arose from where he had been resting. I knew immediately who he was – the great singer-actor Paul Robeson! Seemingly he had accompanied Mrs. Rodd back from one of her Russian forays. I cannot tell you a word of what he said, partly because I was scared to death.

Despite my youth, I had some idea that I might be arrested for hob knobbing with Communists. At the same time I tried to remember what I had heard about Robeson's U.S. citizenship problem so that, if called on, I might make some intelligent remark.

These many years later, I have to wonder if perhaps Mrs. Rodd had brought him here with the thought that her husband might be able to help him with his passport problem. We will likely never know.

As the great man was tired, the evening with him was very short so that he could get some rest. Scared and excited, I caught a bus home. I told no one where I had been or who I had seen since I worried I might be arrested.

I saw Robeson on stage several times afterwards and marvelled that I had actually met such a wonderfully talented man. His Othello with Uta Hagen was memorable.

I'm certain that if Mrs. Leader and Mrs. Rodd were around today they would have been leading protest marches or, at the very least, capably running the city.

As for me, I became a Conservative because my family was. I am told that once as my grandfather and his cousin were leaving the polling booth in Nova Scotia, one struck the other over the head with his cane, saying "you cancelled my vote!" They took politics very seriously in Nova Scotia.

THE CENOTAPH

Recently, I read an article in one of those magazines you see in the beauty salon. It was about the moving of the Windsor Cenotaph and was written by a local woman named Andrea Grimes. There was a photo showing a crowd at the cenotaph when it was located at its original location at the intersection of Ouellette Avenue and Giles Blvd.

I can see it there still, standing rock solid, commanding attention and respect. That picture would have been taken a very long time ago.

Though I couldn't make us out, I knew I was standing to the left of the Cenotaph with my mother and brother. My father was likely marching with a big contingent of WWI veterans. To reach the cenotaph we would have walked west along Giles Boulevard from our home.

It seemed exactly right having the Cenotaph on that corner, commanding all who passed to remember sacrifice and honor due. There were so many parades that passed it; I can recall, not in detail, but in mist as it was in the mid-1920s when I was still a little girl, the gun carriage carrying Col. MacGregor's body as it rumbled down Ouellette Avenue. The crowd stood in complete silence as it passed by.

I also remember when my mother and I walked that route on Giles to see our handsome mayor, Art Reaume, accompany the Duchess of Kent and her daughter, to see the Duchess lay a wreath at the Cenotaph. A few years later my brother-in-law became Aide de Camp to the Duchess.

In May 1937, a huge crowd was assembled on Ouellette Avenue as the city celebrated the ascension of George VI to the throne. Once again I was at the Cenotaph with my mother and brother. My father was on the far side, marching with Branch 12, a little in front, carrying the flag. The parade was proceeding to Jackson Park. Even today I can hear the pipes in the distance and tears spring to my eyes.

After the parade, we met up at home. All seemed well although we were certainly tired. We had walked a great distance, especially my father.

That night he died from a blood clot to the brain. He was just in his 50s – the same age my children are today.

I would soon learn that nothing remains the same. Two young men from our church, Norm Hull and Bill Hunter, who were in fact members of my father's Sunday school class, were sent from the Border Cities Star to do an obituary.

They seemed so young. They sat side by side on the living room chesterfield, not sure of what to ask. Somewhere along the line, Gays River, Nova Scotia, became Goys River, which was a disappointment. Both men rose to senior positions at the paper.

At the funeral, friends who saw my father's last parade further along Ouellette Avenue told us that the veterans were singing "OLD SOLDIERS NEVER DIE", as Legion Branch 12 passed by.

But they do. My father did.

In the 1960s when I was temporarily living in Oakville, I heard Windsor's Cenotaph was to be moved. I couldn't believe the news.

"Why?" I cried. "Why would they do that?"

Then, recalling how strong and solid the monument was, I knew they couldn't move it and that pleased me.

But I was wrong. In 1965, the 106-ton structure was dismantled stone by stone – some weighing 4,300 pounds – and reassembled at its present City Hall location. It was virtually tucked away and became only properly acknowledged once a year – on Remembrance Day.

MY INTRODUCTION TO GREAT THEATRE

I was 19 when WWII began. The boys left and the women went to work.

I was enrolled in a public speaking course at Assumption College.

There was just one other girl in the class and several businessmen. Professor Paulus, a known eccentric, taught the course. We laughed at him and with him, but if I had the sense I do now I would have cherished him. He truly cared about what he was teaching and wanted to broaden our vision.

He got us out of the classroom. We went on walking tours of the then wonderful city of Detroit. We hopped on and off public transit, going from the magnificent Hudson's Department Store downtown, to Christ Church Grosse Pointe where the choir was rehearsing the Dutch Hymn of Thanksgiving for Sunday service.

One day we went to the Cass Theatre, which would soon become my second home. We went to see Walter Hampden and Cecilia Loftus starring in "Arsenic and Old Lace."

After the play ended we were actually invited on stage to meet the stars. I was overcome with awe and couldn't utter a word. The others said very little. As a matter of fact we pretty much stood and stared at the theatre greats. For me it was my first big time production.

Professor Paulus must have forgotten that he was dealing with a dozen people from a small Canadian city. We were aliens, totally different from his New York City milieu. He should have clued us in ahead as to what was expected of us.

Afterwards, he said to me in front of the class, "I was sorely disappointed in you. You didn't say a word. Nothing!"

I have not forgotten how ashamed I was and I regret that he would never know that seeing that play was the catalyst for my life-long love of theatre.

WATCHING BETTE DAVIS

All my life I have read. I cannot stop. When I'm out of new books, or books loaned by friends and haven't a minute to go to Chapters or the library, I turn to Somerset Maugham's anthology of short stories: two volumes, each comprised of some 800 pages.

As this was the case the other night, I started with "Rain" the first story in Volume 1.

As I grow older, I've noticed how certain triggers can send me right back to my past. I began to read and was instantly transported back in time to the old Cass Theatre in Detroit. In those days Broadway-bound plays tried out in Detroit at the Cass or at the Lafayette Theatre across the street. Some would go on to Boston before hitting New York City while others went directly from Detroit.

When WWII broke out so many of the young men on our side of the border had enlisted so it was no trouble for young women to become volunteer ushers, seeing the best of the best theatre, in what was then a thoroughly safe city. It's almost incomprehensible to imagine that about the Detroit of today.

If you were a regular usher at the Cass you could see a play at the Lafayette for free. In fact, that was what I was doing on this particular night.

The ushers would take the tunnel bus from downtown Windsor to Cadillac Square on the American side of the river and walk along Lafayette to the theatre. This was a perfectly safe thing to do, even if you were a young woman alone, which I sometimes was.

That night at the Lafayette, the icon of the theatre, Bette Davis, was trying out the play, "Miss Sadie Thompson". I was there on duty. Bette's husband at that time was Gary Merrill, who walked to and fro across the back of the theatre.

At one point he stopped and said to me, "She knows something is wrong but can't identify it. She wants me to find out what it is."

Whether the play made it in New York or not, I have no idea. I just knew that I was seeing a great actress. And I so wished I could have told Gary Merrill what was wrong.

Many of you will know that "Miss Sadie Thompson" is based on the story of Somerset Maugham's "Rain."

Barbara's mother Mary Theresa (Mollie) Burke MacDonald trained to be a nurse (early 1900s)

Barbara's father, Captain Fred MacDonald, M.C. in WWI

Barbara, her little brother Ian, and mother Mollie in Nova Scotia

Barbara with her mother Mollie in Gays River, Nova Scotia (circa 1920)

Barbara stands with her Grandmother Burke, her mother Mollie and brother Ian in Dumbarton, Scotland

Barbara with her mother Mollie and brother Ian in Alexandria, Scotland

Barbara's brother Ian in his Cub uniform in front of their house on Moy Avenue in Windsor. This was shortly after Barbara, her mother and Ian moved to the city in 1925 to reunite with the children's father.

Barbara's mother Mollie stands at right with Kay Secord (left) and her sister Billie (who married a driver for neighbourhood rumrunner, Bull Fielding) shortly after Barbara and her family arrived in Windsor in 1925.

Barbara (at left) and her friend Arletta at Beckerson's Cottage in Amherstburg, Ontario, early 1930s

Barbara at camp, early 1930s

C.G.I.T. play: Mrs. Apple and her Corps, late 1930s, Windsor, Ontario

Mr. Nichols stands with Barbara's father Fred McDonald (on right) in front of 633 Moy Avenue, Windsor, Ontario, 1930s

Barbara's father Fred MacDonald leading the parade of WWI vets down Ouellette Avenue, Windsor, Ontario, 1930s

Barbara's engagement announcement, Sept. 16, 1947 in the Windsor Daily Star

WINDSOR DAILY STAR, WINDSOR, ONTARIO, TUESDAY, SEPTEMBER 16,

Her Engagement Is Announced

The engagement of Miss Barbara Grant MacDonald, daughter of Mrs. Frederick Grant MacDonald of Windermere road and the late Capt. MacDonald, M. C., to Mr. Leslie Kersey, son of Mr. and Mrs. S. J. Kersey of Esdras place, Riverside, is announced today by her mother, the marriage to take place Saturday afternoon, October 4, at two o'clock, in Chalmers United Church.

Les Kersey stands at right behind chair with his family on the BobLo Boat in the 1920s

Emerson Porter drew these unusual postcards and sent them to his sister Beatrice Porter (Kersey) circa 1900 when she was away working as a mid-wife. She became Barbara's mother-in-law.

Les Kersey swimming at BobLo Island (early 1920s)

The Kersey family stands in front of Belle Isle's magnificent fountain, (Detroit) 1920s

Leslie (left front) and his brother Ken stand in front of their father (with moustache) and uncles, late 1920s

Dan Dunlop and Ron Clayton (front) and Les Kersey (top left), the boys from Gladstone Avenue and Ontario Street (Walkerville) about 1939

Les Kersey stands at the left of Doug McNale in downtown Windsor, early 1940s

MENTAL ILLNESS:
Why My Mother Was "Different"

I can't say when I realized that my mother was unlike other mothers. She was unpredictable and often angry. As I lay in my bed at night, unable to sleep, I would think about my family. I blamed my mother's strange behaviour on a number of things: my Irish Grandfather, whom no one knew, the Catholic thing, possibly the Presbyterians, or maybe it could have been the hard life on a Canadian farm.

Or maybe my parents just didn't like each other any more.

When our father died my mother didn't say a word to us about the loss; no hugs or kisses. She had lain in bed for a couple of days face to the wall, and I deduced she felt remorse for the difficult life she had given him. Then she got up and he was buried from the church (not something the United Church generally did). She then went to the basement and tore up his writings, his drawings, even tossed out a couple of small tables he had made. Everything went in the garbage.

When she had gone through the small insurance, she took an abrupt turn in her thinking. Now she had been married to the greatest man ever! We had to listen to her extol his virtues, his bravery. It was sickening to me since I knew how he had been treated. She would even interrupt conversations to throw in a word or two about his devotion to duty, his good manners, his fine family – anything and everything.

Next she cast her eye on my brother and for the rest of her life, was completely absorbed with spreading word of his greatness.

I was the one she chose to hate. She found fault with everything I did and constantly criticized me for the rest of her long life. I was subjected to her harassing phone calls even while I was at work.

A short while after my father had died, my mother told me, "You're coming with me." We went to see a doctor, not the family doc as he might tell someone in the congregation, but to a former Cape Breton acquaintance of my father's. My mother explained to him very clearly that she could not get a grip on herself, that she flew off the handle and that she needed help.

Without checking any of her vitals, the doctor said, "You're fine Mrs. Mac. Just buy a bottle scotch and tie one on. You'll be ok."

There was never any liquor in our home and I knew that the doctor's off hand reply was no answer to what my mother rightly perceived was a problem.

I know now that she was probably bipolar, at the very least. But no one knew that word then. Now I understand that a pill, maybe even just Valium, would have helped her, but family doctors back then had no knowledge of such an illness let alone medication for it.

I longed to have a loving mother and to be a loving daughter, but that was not possible.

When my father was alive, he had learned early on that he couldn't win so he just ignored her outbursts, or, left the house to pursue one of his hobbies.

My father may have been a smart man, valiant in battle, but he just couldn't cope with my mother. She was so demanding. When she was pregnant with my brother and I, her mother had to be brought from Scotland. This was no small feat in a 1920 winter in rural Nova Scotia. As grandmother couldn't miss Sunday mass and there was no Catholic churches nearby, a driver had to be found to take her to the one in a Dutch Settlement each Sunday.

Whatever her mental problem, she could stop in a tirade and be as pleasant and sane as anyone else. In those days you didn't have to phone to see if it was convenient to visit. You just went to the door and knocked. On one such occasion a lady of prominence in Walkerville called when my mother was in the midst of an angry fit. My mother opened the door, smiled, greeted the woman warmly, served her tea and they had a chat. When the lady left my mother resumed her tirade exactly where it had been interrupted. Isn't that strange? I've often thought of that moment.

Once, in desperation, I went to a woman of influence and told her some of what was going on. After some thought, she said, "I cannot help you." I later learned there were no laws to help children and you couldn't just put someone away who you suspected had mental problems.

As a grown woman and mother, I learned that I was not the only one suffering. One of my best friends confessed they had gone through the same thing but her father had been a buffer, making it easier. Another time a local merchant told me of his home troubles and his wife was acting just like my mother. He was the buffer between her and the children. It gave me some comfort but Ian and I had our buffer – our father, for such a short time.

Once, listening to some talk show, I heard the late actor Tony Curtis describing what had gone on in his home when he was growing up. I was transfixed. He could have been describing our home. This started me thinking. Is this some kind of mental problem that affects only women? What is it called?

A couple of years ago my brother intimated that he did not think our mother loved him. "Are you crazy," I replied, "She had no other subject of conversation but you her last few years. She loved you. She told everyone."

He said, quietly, "She never told me."

THE IRISH TROUBLES

Recently, a young doctor (they all look young enough to be my grandchildren) introduced himself to me at the eye doctors. His last name was Scottish so I asked if it was spelled with an "Mc" or a "Mac". I explained that my grandmother, a McKeen, told me that the McKeens had originally been MacDonald's before fleeing Scotland for the north of Ireland. This was probably shortly after the Massacre of Glencoe in 1692 when the Campbells, who had accepted their hospitality, killed 38 MacDonalds from the Clan MacDonald of Glencoe.

It was then that my grandmother's family changed their name to McKeen.

The doctor sad he had exactly the same background and that according to his aunt our families had triggered the Irish troubles.

"How?!" I asked. This was astonishing news.

He explained, "My aunt told me that it was due to bringing the Protestant religion to a Catholic country."

I was left dumbfounded. Had my ancestors really helped start the Irish Troubles that continue to this day?

There had been many, many MacDonalds in our neighbourhood when I was growing up. One day a letter the mailman had just delivered was addressed to different MacDonalds. My mother looked out and could see the mailman several doors along the other side of the street.

"Run and give this back to him," she said. When I returned she asked, "What did he say?"

"They should have done a better job at Glencoe," I replied.

A REAL EDUCATION

It was when exams started in my third year at Kennedy Collegiate that my father died from a blood clot to the brain. In those years, we were graded academically. I did pass that year, but not well, which surprised me as I had taken the class pin the year before for standing first. I always stood well.

It was the chemistry class that did it. I knew when the year began that it was not a subject for me. I should have taken German, which was the alternative, but as Hitler was in the news daily and public opinion was running against Germany, I somehow felt it would be disloyal to take that class. I guess I can blame Adolph Hitler for my poor mark in chemistry.

When my father died, our social network clicked in again. Mr. McNaughton, principal of Walkerville Collegiate, and Mr. Davidson, Principal of King Edward School, suggested to my mother that Ian and I be sent to Walkerville Collegiate so they could keep a fatherly eye on us. The men were both elders and shared the duties of running the Sunday school at our church.

At home there was almost no money coming in and my mother did not work (more about this later) nor would she accept welfare. After all, she was a Scot. So it fell to me to do something. I left Walkerville Collegiate at the end of my fourth year and so began my love affair with downtown Windsor.

My mother approached Legion Branch 12 and boldly suggested that in memory of my father they pay my way to Windsor Business College. I knew nothing of this until later and when I was working I was glad to be able to pay them back somewhat for their kindness. My friend Dorothy Roach also enrolled.

At that time downtown Windsor was as exciting to me as New York City. I was living on Lincoln Road near the Detroit River then and Dorothy lived in the red brick house on the northeast corner of Devonshire and Wyandotte. In the morning, we would chat on the phone and then leave our homes at about the same time to meet each other on Wyandotte at Chilver to take the streetcar downtown.

We would hop off at the stop on the west side of Ouellette between Chatham and University then race up the College's old wooden stairs to the second floor and into a lecture room with a bank of windows overlooking Ouellette Avenue. There was another room full of typewriters. We learned bookkeeping, shorthand and typing and no one fooled around. We were there to learn and we did.

Below the school was a Woolworth's and another dime store, as they were called, which I believe was Kresge's. At noon we scurried down the stairs with our lunch bags, hurrying to get a seat at the Woolworth's counter as my friend Mitzi worked there. For a nickel we got a wonderful milk shake and Mitzi made sure we got our nickel's worth.

Other friends I especially remember from that class were Mary Chittim, Doris Wilson and Blanche Teahan. Dorothy became the poet Dorothy Farmiloe. I am still in touch with Blanche and Doris. Blanche's aunt, Mrs. Egan, was head of Ladies Sports Wear at C. H. Smith Department Store downtown and we all thought that was so cool.

Even though the Depression was still on and consequently there were no jobs, this reality never entered my mind. I worked hard and graduated in May 1939 to a changing world. War was in the air; Germany was on the move.

WORKING GIRL

The timing of my graduation was fortuitous. The Depression was about to end and there would soon be more jobs than there were people looking for work.

Bendix Eclipse called the College for help and I was sent, beginning work immediately on the reception desk and the switchboard. "Have you any experience?" was what I was told to ask the people flowing in seeking work.

One day after I asked this stock question to a tall, rangy and angry young man, he bent over the desk and hissed in my ear, "How can I get experience if I can't get a job?" I was completely on his side. He represented the frustration of a generation and I would know him later as Windsor Mayor Frank Wansborough.

That same year WWII was declared. Canada was at war again and the landscape of our lives would change forever. The old Burroughs building on St. Luke Road was swiftly turned into a recruitment centre and barracks. Early on I saw our mayor, Private David Croll, standing guard duty on the east side of the building, body rigid, eyes straight ahead.

Recruits were at times marched to and from the barracks along Ottawa Street. They were just boys. Husbands and brothers began leaving and then the first casualties appeared in the paper. My own brother, underage, was gone in a moment. It all happened so fast I wondered how those in charge of the war effort could get into action so speedily.

At Bendix I moved along to become secretary to the Purchasing Agent Harry Cole. I really liked him and we had things in common, including the fact that both our brothers were German prisoners of war. And I liked my job until one day the young man who cashed our pay cheques (banks then closed at 3 p.m. and were not open on weekends) came in and said something like, "Betty makes more than you do."

I was astounded for I worked long hours without much pay. I immediately quit.

I knew exactly what my mother would say for she was dependent on some of my pay. And she didn't disappoint. She seethed! She was actually so distraught that she called Mr. Philip Adams who of course went to our church and was Chief Engineer of Canadian Bridge to tell him what I had done.

How embarrassing! There was often no rhyme nor reason for her actions.

At this time Aircraft Hydraulics (a member of the Bendix family) was getting into production of aircraft parts and Lou Maunder, the general manager, happened to be downtown for a meeting when he met a Mr. G. Murray Gossage. Mr. Gossage had been demobilized from the army and asked to go to Windsor and open an office for the Aluminum Company of Canada.

Aluminum was especially needed in wartime and a lot of the work was being done in Windsor. Mr. Gossage told him of his needs for a soon-to-be-opened sales office. Mr. Maunder said to Mr. Gossage, "You want Miss Macdonald."

Mr. Gossage called me and I was soon traveling to Aluminum Company plants in Etobicoke to see how the castings were made and then on to Kingston to look at the sheet mill.

We settled into offices in the Canada Building on Ouellette near Park Street. After the war ended in 1945, I had a front row seat at the window when the Essex Scottish Regiment returned, marching triumphantly down Ouellette Avenue, pipes playing, kilts swaying.

Downtown was such a lively place then and working in the core put me once again in the heart of things. My war years were busy and spent in essential work. When a granddaughter visited a few of years ago and said "What did you do in the war, Nan?" I was nonplussed. That was a question they used to ask men.

But, like everyone else, I worked hard, gave blood regularly, knitted socks for service men (heaven help whoever got mine) and, for some reason I marched for a while with the Red Cross inside the old Ferry building which stood on the Detroit River at the foot of Ouellette Avenue.

Men in uniform on leave were around on weekends, visiting relatives, or on course in the area.

How we danced. We danced at the Y, at the Masonic Temple where I saw my first zoot-suiters, and at Coral Gables. Feeling very elegant we sat at small tables in the Norton Palmer Hotel or danced until we dropped. Towards the end of the war we spent time at Thomas's Inn on the Detroit River east of Windsor near Tecumseh, dancing and falling in and out of love. And always we danced to a live orchestra.

And then one day the war was over.

In January 1947 I was sounded out about a position as secretary to the new American Advertising Manager of Hiram Walker.

Hiram Walker was very different then. It was much posher and was truly a place of privilege – expensive wood panelling, thick carpets, ivy covered walls and it was still locally owned. The senior executives ate in the executive dining room at 1 p.m. and we few secretaries gathered in the cafeteria, ate, played bridge and became lifelong friends. And we knew the Presidents who were well liked as they treated everyone the same. I still think of Tommy Gibbons and Cliff Hatch; they were part of our Windsor lives.

(I still see co-workers from those days: Peggy Coulter who married Dr. Bill Foster and I am best friend to Pat Sunstrum who became Mrs. L. L. Odette.)

BECOMING A KERSEY

While I was ushering at the Cass Theatre in Detroit one evening, a tall, fair and handsome young man approached me. We chit chatted for a while and then he asked me out to see a play. His name was Les Kersey and he was playing Ben in the Windsor Theatre Guild's production of the Little Foxes at Walkerville Collegiate.

I would have said I had never seen him before but he was from Windsor so there's a good chance I had. Not only was he a good actor, he had a calm disposition and was well liked. Then Les and I dated and decided to get married on October 4, 1947.

One day in September of that same year my boss phoned for me to come in to his office. I grabbed a note pad and pen and trotted down the hushed carpeted hall.

Mr. Swan was an American from their wine subsidiary W. A. Taylor in New York, and he commuted between New York and Grosse Pointe. (Advertising for the 'white goods', vodka and gin, was handled by C. J. La Roche Advertising of New York.)

In the room that day was the ad company's president, Mr. LaRoche, and account executive Mr. Pratt. I smiled and then my boss said, "Miss Macdonald is getting married on Saturday and going to New York on her honeymoon."

Mr. LaRoche stood up and shook hands with me, wished me well and then asked if I would accept the use of his family's apartment in the Waldorf Towers for the week. I nearly fell down right there and of course I accepted without even calling my husband-to-be, Les Kersey.

As he had been to New York in 1939 for the World's Fair, Les had assured me there were hotels galore, but his attempts to find one for our honeymoon had been fruitless. The offer of the suite in the Waldorf Towers was unbelievably wonderful.

Was I ever lucky!

I can't remember exactly how long it took to drive to New York but it was hours and hours. It was after midnight when we arrived and Times

Square was lit up and was as bright as day. The Waldorf Towers was maybe the best address in the world. When we pulled up in our old 1939 black sedan I nearly died when the doorman stepped forward and opened my door. Pop cans rolled out and there were sandwich wrappers littering the seats. He didn't bat an eye as he escorted me from the car.

Mr. LaRoche's sister-in-law was the Hollywood actress Rosalind Russell! There were several pictures of her in the Waldorf apartment and we presumed she used the apartment on occasion.

Mr. Pratt, a VP of the ad agency phoned the next morning with their suggestions for things to do but said he didn't want to interfere with our plans. I told him it was no problem. We ended up going to the Plaza for dinner that night, another night to "21" where I saw my first TV, and another time to the races which Mr. Pratt really enjoyed.

Les had booked tickets for the ball game and to "Annie Get your Gun" with Ethel Merman. We had good seats for the musical because that would be Les's priority and I wish I could remember who was playing at the ball game (Les would have remembered for it was October and into the world series).

Our favourite place that trip was the Rainbow Room at the top of Rockefeller Plaza. We would return there many times over the years.

I can truly say it was a dream beginning to a wonderful married life.

Les's parents, Sydney and Beatrice Kersey, had come to Canada from the South of England sometime during, or just before WWI. They settled in Hamilton but then moved to Windsor where his father, who was a cabinetmaker, began work on the Fox Theatre in Detroit, which was only a mile away across the river. When the Depression hit no one could afford a cabinetmaker so he was out of work.

Les's sister Dora, who was 10 years older, was a champion swimmer with what I believe was called the Border Cities Swim Club. She had elocution lessons and was in demand for readings at local Windsor clubs. She knew all of the English Albert Ramsbottom comedic routines, which were so popular in the 1930s and her daughter, Babs Holdsworth, still recites them to this day. Ken could recite many of them as well.

Dora was active in local theatre productions. One particular night during a performance, she was to die on the sofa. She collapsed on cue and closed her eyes, the curtain closed (or so she thought) and she jumped up. The whole audience burst into laughter. The curtain had been caught on the end of the sofa so everyone could see her "resurrection".

Another night she was on stage holding a baby when the baby reached up, grabbed her necklace and yanked, sending beads helter skelter all over the stage. She said it was chaos – actors trying to say their lines, while trying not to step on beads and especially, trying not to laugh.

Dora met a man named Fred Brown on the ferryboat that ran between Windsor and Detroit. They married and by the time she was 21, Dora was a mother and living in Hamilton. Fred became head of the Westinghouse Bulb Division, and during the height of the Depression, he and Dora took in her whole family: mother, father, and her 2 brothers, Les and Ken; and they in turn never forgot this kindness.

Sometime after their mother died when Les was 16 the Kersey men decided to move back to Windsor. His brother Ken went to work at Hiram Walker's & Sons Distillery. He also became Lt. Col. of the Essex Scottish, worked with the Theatre Guild and on community fundraisers. His wife Gladys was the first person I ever met with Multiple Sclerosis.

Grandfather Brown, Fred's father (also named Fred) was a first cousin to the English comedienne and actress Bea Lilley (originally from Toronto she became Lady Peel when she married Sir Robert Peel). The Browns and Lilleys are buried in Walsham Le Willows cemetery near Cornwall, England.

Les's father found work at Ford Motor and married fun loving Mrs. Speirs. Les had stayed in Hamilton to finish his schooling and then came back to Windsor.

During that time, Ken went to the Dominion Drama Festival in Ottawa with the Windsor Theatre Guild's production of Night Must Fall. Robert Montgomery and Rosalind Russell were in the Oscar winning 1937 movie. I think Windsor did well this time.

MARITAL BLISS

We replaced Les's 1939 Ford as soon as we could. Our beautiful new light blue Ford 4-door sedan cost $3000 and because we were both working and saving, we paid cash which floored our salesman at Webster Motors in downtown Windsor.

Then we started saving again, this time for a down payment on a house. Skimping was no problem for us, having come through the Depression. In around 1950 we built a house, doing a lot of the work ourselves. All of our friends were doing exactly the same thing.

Then the officials of the Windsor Theatre Guild asked me and then pleaded with me to get involved in the organization. I did not realize how perfectly this would suit me so I was resistant. When I finally agreed to participate the people who graciously greeted me were known to me from the social pages of the paper and therefore I was intimidated. As well, I had the distinct impression that I would be expected to start emoting immediately. If only they had explained that I could be behind scenes, sweeping, prompting, but they didn't. When I discovered I was not expected to be on stage, my relief was profound.

And along came our children: Grant, Sheila and then my third Mark due at Christmas time in 1956. I was admitted to Met Hospital for an unexpected caesarean, while Les had a terrible cold and my mother was in Grace Hospital with pneumonia. Friends Jack and Peg Fuller decorated my room with a lovely Christmas tree and then Les was spirited away to play piano at a party at the Reaume's, which was nearby. A taxi had to be sent to the Fuller House to pick up Jack's trombone as he had arrived at the party without it. The taxi driver said it was the first time he had a trombone for a fare. I wonder if my doctor Tom Robson remembers this.

WHAT I KNOW ABOUT MULTIPLE SCLEROSIS

I got to know Gladys Kersey when I married Les for she was his brother's wife and my sister-in-law. That was in 1947. Gladys told me that growing up in Ridgetown as part of the Silcox family she twice fell to the ground as her leg buckled under her. The doctor could find no apparent reason for this and prescribed bed rest.

Eventually she came to Windsor to live and work. She met and married Ken Kersey and they had a little girl, Karen. Then the awful MS hit. Mega. When I met her she was in a wheel chair but more often in bed. Before our meeting she had been to the Mayo Clinic in Minnesota and lived the rest of her life on the diet they prescribed. Ken picked up her bread at Adler's on Drouillard road and she absolutely could not touch eggs.

At this time there were no Government health programs. To make ends meet, Ken worked during the week at Hiram Walker's and Saturdays at Trott's Shoes on Ouellette Avenue. After work, he would strap roller skates on Gladys and then stand at the end of the bed with a board while rolling her legs up and down the board in an effort to strengthen them. Despite these trials and tribulations, Ken always seemed in good humour but it must have been difficult. His sister Dora returned to Windsor for a while to help out.

When I entered the family Gladys would sometimes travel by ambulance for assessment and treatment in Detroit. In those days the average citizen had not heard of this disease. Gladys chose not to have the aggressive treatment advised, although the two other Windsorites also stricken with MS, (one of whom I remember as Hugh Paulin), who travelled in the ambulance with her, did. Gladys lived to old age while, unfortunately, the others died young.

When she was well enough to take in a bit of a regimental party at the Windsor Armouries, two officers would cross their arms and make a seat with their hands and lifted Gladys up the front steps for there was no elevator.

A DIFFERENT KIND OF WORK

The years from 1939 to 1949 comprised my so-called working life. Afterwards, I stayed home to raise a family, which is the way it was done in those days.

I acknowledge the fine work done by our women in uniform, but this is written from my perspective. Marjorie Harvey and Kitty Hare were my only women friends who enlisted.

I never seemed to stop getting involved in things.

It started when Mr. Gossage's wife arrived in Windsor during the war years. She had lots of social connections and was soon asked to take on a section of Welcome Wagon. She couldn't type so lured me in to doing this for her. After all, her husband was my boss.

She made her Welcome Wagon calls and then came to my home once a week to dictate the information. She was what one called the outdoors type, a big likeable woman who paced up and down, smoking and dictating in our small living room. My mother was mesmerized by it all.

When I retired and the Gossage's left Windsor I was urged to take on her WW calls and decided I could do that. Eventually I was in charge of most of Southwestern Ontario and it boggles my mind when I think of it. That's how I met Dr. Cam and Katie Macdonald and a lot of other wonderful people.

OAKVILLE YEARS

Les was employed in Ford Canada's office for his whole working life. We were moved to Oakville in 1959 for his job and the family blossomed and we were all very active. Les would hoot if he could read this for we had a busy life in Windsor. But I'm not wrong.

In Oakville, Les sang in St. John's United Church choir, and he curled. I taught Sunday school and I'll never forget when our minister, Rev. Jim Terry of St. John's United Church, came to call and somewhere in our conversation I said something unusually stupid.

Remembering the turmoil my mother caused, I said, "I make a point of never giving in to anger."

He replied, "What about righteous indignation?"

Talk about a great comeback.

I joined the board of the Y and the family joined the Oakville Club and Les got to play a lot of golf. The children made friends and Grant was declared a gifted student. It was at that point that I was asked to take on a huge territory for Welcome Wagon.

Life was going along well when, after about six years away from Windsor, we were sent back. It was upsetting to have our lovely life in Oakville interrupted, but we never looked behind us.

HOME AGAIN

Only two houses in Walkerville, our preferred neighbourhood in Windsor, were for sale within our price bracket. Walkerville had the church, the library, the schools, shopping nearby and the bus. It was the perfect location for raising a family.

Les was working night and day on some project whereby export documentation was being transferred to Windsor from Ford New Jersey. As he was so busy, I set about getting the family reestablished in Windsor.

I soon learned that if you've been away for a few years the ranks have closed and it's work finding your place again.

So back to our social network: the church, the symphony, theatre and the curling club. The Windsor Symphony was directed by Matti Holli and ensconced at the Tivoli Theatre on Wyandotte Street in Walkerville. Les purchased five season tickets but the children put up an awful fuss when they had to attend. Their only delight on those Sunday evenings was to rush forward at intermission to kibitz with the trombonist, our friend Dr. Jack Fuller.

Maj. K.S. Kersey Named Commander of Scottish

Maj. Kenneth S. Kersey, C.D., has been named to command the Essex and Kent Scottish Regiment upon the retirement of Lt. Col. A. J. Hodges, M.C., C.D., on Jan. 15.

The announcement was made Thursday by Col. Hodges who had been advised of the appointment by Army Headquarters in Ottawa and authorized to make the announcement in Windsor.

Major Kersey has been second in command of the regiment since November, 1951. At the time the unit was known as the Essex Scottish Regiment. He assumes command on Monday, Jan. 16.

In October, 1954, when the Essex Scottish and the Kent Regiment of Chatham were amalgamated to form the Essex and Kent Scottish Regiment, Major Kersey was reappointed as second in command.

A change of command parade will be held at the Windsor Armories on Jan. 27, at which time the Chatham Garrison will parade in Windsor.

Col. Hodges assumed command of the Essex Scottish Regiment in November, 1951, from Lt.-Col. Walter L. McGregor. He remained as C.O. of the regiment until amalgamation with the Kent Regiment in October, 1954, and then became the first commanding officer of the newly formed Essex and Kent Scottish Regi-

See MAJ. KERSEY—Page 6

MAJ. K. S. KERSEY, C.D.
... regimental leader

Barbara's brother-in-law Major Ken Kersey when he was named Commander of the Essex and Kent Scottish Regiment, January 1955

Barbara and her husband Les Kersey (at right) stand with the Honourable George Drew, 14th Premier of Ontario (1943 to 1948) and leader of the Progressive Conservative Party (1948 to 1956), and Mr. and Mrs. Warren A. Bolton. Mr. Bolton was head of the Windsor Utilities Commission.

Hiram Walker's Players & Glee Club program for "Foam on the Range", an original story by employees Ken Kersey (Barbara's brother-in-law), Sam Barker, Bill Arison and Larry Renaud. Produced by Ken Kersey and Bill Arison, 1950s. Ken also played "Hoot Owl" in the performance.

WINDSOR THEATRE GUILD

presents

"*Post Road*"

A Mystery Comedy

by

Wilbur Daniel Steele and Norma Mitchell

DIRECTED BY—DOUG BAKE

Production Manager—Gloria Clarke

SYNOPSIS OF SCENES

Act 1
Scene 1—An evening in October.
Scene 2—One week later - morning.

Act 2
Scene 1—Early evening of the same day.
Scene 2—Fifteen minutes later.

The action of the play takes place in the living room of Emily Madison's home in Connecticut.

Cast

George Preble	Doug Bake
May Madison Preble	Vera Lugce
Wesley Cartwright	Ed Tomkins
Bill	Tom Downey
Celia	June Pearce
Emily Madison	Dorothy A. Taylor
Jeeby Cashier	Winnie Jolly
Dr. Spender	Les Kersey
Nurse Martin	Evelyn Kerr
The Girl	Margaret Patterson
Matt	Marshall Romanik
Virgil Bemis	Robert Walton
Mrs. Cashier	Dorothy Graham
Mrs. Canby	Reta Mills
Announcer	James Benton

ACKNOWLEDGEMENTS

Box Office	Evangeline Robbins, Norman Jenkins, Anthony Turner
Staging	Tom Downey
Stage Crew	Valda Turner, Sam Graham, Frank Scully
Lighting	Douglas Laing
House Manager	Virginia DeLaurier
Properties	Alvira Brush, Ruth Merson, Cora McCulloch
Make-up	Jack Bickle
Publicity	Valerie Kasurak
Music	C.K.L.W. Ensemble
Costumes	C. H. Smith Co., Bartlet Macdonald and Gow Gertrude Arnold
Furniture	Peter Tinning, Rana Hall, Birks and Sons

Windsor Theatre Guild program for "Post Road", which played at Walkerville Collegiate, was the last production of 1946-47 season 27. Les Kersey was "Dr. Spender"

Les, Barbara and their children (l-r Grant, Sheila and Mark) on opening night of Windsor Light Opera Association's production of Oliver!, Cleary Auditorium, 1966

"When the Progressive Conservative Party enters a candidate for Provincial Parliament who has the outstanding ability and fine character of Mrs. Barbara Kersey, I am delighted to be first to sign her nomination" said Mrs. Cameron Montrose, former member of City Council (shown on right with Mrs. Kersey). "I'm betting on Barbara!"

Barbara with Mrs. Cameron Montrose, the first person to sign her nomination paper for member of Provincial Parliament, Windsor/Walkerville riding, 1971

Barbara with husband Les in her campaign office, 1971

Renée Bondy (above), Barbara's friend and at one time her next door neighbour, composed a musical based on her four children called, "We All Want", performed as a successful fund raiser for Windsor's second Art in the Park in the early 1970s. The program cover was also designed by Renée.

HANDICRAFTS—Mrs. Fran Odell (left) and Mrs. Barbara Kersey, business partners in a handicraft shop in downtown Windsor which opened Tuesday, examine a few of their wares.

2 'idea people' open outlet for area artisans, hobbyists

By SUSAN VAN KUREN

"We are both idea people," said Barbara Kersey gesturing toward her business partner Fran Odell. "She's right. You can almost see light-bulbs in their eyes."

In an enthusiastic attempt to further local handicraft, the two women have opened an outlet for the work of Windsor and Essex County hobbyists and artisans at 6 Riverside we'll create a little excitement downtown," added Mrs. Odell.

The two women emphasized that while the business aspect of their endeavor is definitely present, nevertheless, they want to bring creative people together.

Eventually, they hope to have a bulletin board listing artistic functions going on in the area and brochures of places to go. point, paintings, candles, ceramics, dolls and novelties of various types. But they expect a lot more to come.

Beginning Saturday, a flea market will be conducted outside, at the rear of the hotel.

Partners Fran Odell (left) and Barbara in the "Bazaar", a pottery boutique they founded and ran in the British American Hotel in the 1970s (northeast corner of Riverside Drive and Ouellette Avenue, Windsor)

World's Biggest Garage Sale, cartoon by Bob Monks, appeared in
The Windsor Star in the early 1970s

Our Business Is Bringing Your Business To Windsor

Take a good look at one of our country's brightest economic centres right in the very beginning of Canada. Talk to the friendly, hardworking people who made it that way. You'll see how they became involved.

Consider that last year tourism and convention spending totalled $100 million. Retail sales were the best ever at $686 million and industrial investments of more than $159 million contributed greatly to one of the lowest unemployment levels in the country.

With the resources available to our organizations we can provide you with the latest comprehensive information on our economic picture as it is today and what we are projecting for the future.

With our connections, we can put you in touch with the right people for development or investment opportunities.

In short, working through one of our agencies enables all of us to work together for the benefit of good business. And in Windsor, good business is booming.

Barbara when she was Secretary Manager for the Windsor Business Association, 1970s

Barbara Kersey

Barbara Kersey, wife of Les Kersey, Windsor Export Supply, has a wide range of community interests which have always included the promotion of the arts. This year she is chairman of Windsor's annual "Art In The Park" festival.

For some years, she has been a member of the Progressive Conservative Association, both federal and provincial, and last October she was the Conservative candidate in the riding of Windsor-Walkerville. A week before the awards dinner, she was elected president of her riding association.

Mrs. Kersey has also been active with the Y.M.-Y.W.C.A. as a member of the governing board, as a member of the national public relations committee and, currently, as a fund-raiser in the Windsor Y's building fund campaign.

She is secretary of the Old Walkerville association; a former member of the I.O.D.E.; and a former member of the Riverside Arena fund-raising team. She also teaches Sunday school at Chalmers United Church.

May, 1972 4   5 May, 1972

Symphony job for Kersey

By Harry van Vugt
Star Staff Reporter

The board of directors of the Windsor Symphony Society was expected to formally ratify the appointment of Barbara Kersey as the orchestra's business manager at a meeting scheduled this afternoon.

Mrs. Kersey, manager of the Central Windsor Development Corporation for five years, resigned from that post Monday.

Her predecessor with the symphony (but with the title of secretary-manager) was G. William Richardson, who resigned effective April 30.

The appointment of Mrs. Kersey means that the Windsor Symphony now has a new music director (Laszlo Gatti), new business manager and will also have new office quarters in the near future.

Mrs. Kersey is to begin her new job May 15 — also when the symphony hopes to move into new quarters on the third floor of the Toronto Dominion Bank building at Wyandotte Street and Ouellette Avenue. The symphony now shares space with the Windsor Federation of Musicians at 682 Ouellette.

Richard Householder, chairman of the symphony's managerial search committee, said advertising for the job attracted 21 formal applications plus several other enquiries ranging from Vancouver to Prince Edward Island.

"I feel that we had a good cross section," he said.

Among the qualities considered were managerial skills, experience in fund raising and an understanding of arts organizations.

"She met all of those criteria."

Householder also cited her "dynamic personality and high profile" in the community. "We feel that the symphony's position is enhanced by having her associated with us."

Mrs. Kersey admitted she's a novice when it comes to music: "I am probably the least musical person in town but my family is all musical.

"That is not what I'm hired for."

She said she particularly
CONTINUED on Page 4

BARBARA KERSEY
...now in music business

"We've done it", symphony says

WINDSOR — Although she is leaving her position as secretary-manager of the Windsor Symphony June 30, Barbara Kersey and Music Director and Conductor Lazlo Gatti have put together a symphony team Windsor can be proud of.

Barbara joined the symphony exactly one year ago following a five year stint as secretary-manager of the Central Windsor Development corporation. When she accepted the symphony post Barbara said she knew her main task would be to build and organize.

"We've done it," she said. "They didn't even have a mailing list before." The first six to eight months she put in 8:00 a.m. to 8:00 p.m. days. The job still entails seven days per week but the hours have been shortened to 9:00 a.m. to 6:00 p.m. "It absorbs and consumes your life," she said. "Fortunately my husband is a classical music buff."

Weekends are hectic as well. When a Sunday
Continued on Page 24

Above: Announcement in the Windsor Star regarding Barbara's Windsor Symphony Business Manager position (1979)

Barbara with Windsor Symphony maestro Lazlo Gatti, 1980

WINDSOR SYMPHONY — Music director and conductor, Lazlo Gatti and Secretary-Manager Barbara Kersey of the Windsor Symphony Orchestra have put together a vibrant symphony team. Mrs. Kersey will soon be leaving the

Barbara with Danni Bobb (top left) and Marc Dubois at grand opening of the new Art Gallery of Windsor, February 2001

Barbara's brother Lt. Col Ian MacDonald, passed away while she was writing her book

DOWNTOWN WINDSOR IN THE 1970S

Filled with a vibrant mix of shops and restaurants downtown was a special place to spend time dining and shopping. Enthusiastic local people who really cared about the city managed these shops.

At one time I knew the store names on Ouellette Avenue from Park St. north to University Avenue by heart. I can still recall many: Birks Jewelry anchoring the corner of Park, then Dak's Shoes, the Gold Shop, McCance Ladies Wear, Peter Ryan's selling high end gifts and silver, Esquire Men's Wear and then Montreal Trust. As a matter of fact that whole block was elite. The Cherniak family owned Thrifty's Men's Wear on the northeast corner of Ouellette and University.

I just can't seem to remember the name of the gourmet shop that was across the street and next to Maggie's Dress Shop; they had amazing cheeses.

I can't take credit for much but I take full credit for launching the parking garage at Chatham St. and Goyeau Ave. when I was head of the Downtown Business Association. People simply refused to use the parking garage and Eric Wiley, the man in charge, was at a loss as to what to do. I came up with the idea of CANADA'S BIGGEST GARAGE SALE and citizens rented all the spaces and sold everything under the sun. The event was a huge success and I still have Bob Monk's Windsor Star cartoon of a gloating me standing in front of the garage, quipping "Now that we've got them all downtown, let's lock the door!"

Anyone who has worked in a downtown atmosphere knows how exciting it can be and also how frustrating, how kind and smart the merchants are, and how precarious their income can be. Windsor is on the brink of enormous change and for the most part, change is good. However, I venture to say there will not be the colourful people who inhabited our downtown 30 years ago. I was lucky enough to be there. Let me tell you of just a few.

Jack Shanfield

He was not a big man and did not stand out in a crowd. He always seemed to be squinting through his dark rimmed glasses. But he was smart and a force to be reckoned with in downtown Windsor. He and his wife were well known figures in the city as the owners of Shanfield's, a large jewellery and china shop at the corner of Ouellette Avenue and Chatham Street.

I met him right after I became head of the Downtown Business Association. The merchants had tried to pass a law at City Hall to form a BIA, or "Business Improvement Area". Each business was assessed a sum that would be used for beautification purposes, etc. and a certain number of businesses had to agree or the law could not be passed. It had failed in Windsor because Jack had mounted opposition and had enough strength on his side to stop it.

"Who voted against it?" I asked, ready to do battle with them.

"The Tunnel Corporation," I was told. It seemed the Detroit/Windsor Tunnel Corporation owned enough of downtown to stop this law from being passed and Jack had recruited them to his side.

After talking to the Tunnel executives and determining that if it came to a vote again, they would still oppose it, Art Webber and I sat down with the map of the city and zoned out the tunnel. It made a strange eastern border for downtown but the legislation passed.

Before it came into effect, and it was not overnight, I had moved along to become manager of the Windsor Symphony. I ran into Jack in the post office. "You made a mistake by leaving," he said. "The business association has money now and the new head is getting a decent salary."

He was right about that. I made a big mistake.

The whole time I was with the Downtown, Jack seemed to be in opposition to any idea. We'd be at city council for approval of something or other and Jack would be turn up and speak against us.

Over thirty years later, I ran into him in the eye laser clinic at Hotel Dieu Hospital. We were sitting in a long line waiting for his or her turn. I saw Jack and got up to speak to him. "What are you doing?" demanded a volunteer. "Get back in the line."

At 90 years of age I won't be pushed around, so I said, "I'm talking to an old friend," and continued to chat with Jack. And I was glad I did for he died soon after our – for once – peaceful meeting.

Art Webber

Art was a tall, thin, wiry man whose sharp features bore no resemblance to the man he actually was. He was delightful to know. Art was clever, funny, hardworking and possessed an independent mind. Art owned the north side of Chatham Street between the alley behind Shanfield's to the alley before the parking garage. His main company was Windsor Electric but he also owned the hardware store.

For years a number of downtown businesses closed on Wednesday afternoons. The Association thought they should all be open to appeal to tourists so I asked him one day to consider staying open on Wednesday afternoons like merchants did at the Devonshire Mall.

"No way," he snapped. "If I wanted to keep mall hours, I'd be at the mall."

Gus Salidas

Gus was a small, warm, pudgy Greek man who owned a newspaper shop on Ouellette Avenue immediately north of the Canada Building. He also had books for sale. Gus was always eager to promote his homeland and we loved his enthusiasm and his invitations to dinner on Greek holidays.

I was told that Gus would go to Texas to get books and magazines for his shop, and somehow return the same day. In 1971, he became famous for bringing Xaviera Hollander, New York City's leading madam to Windsor to promote her book, "The Happy Hooker: My Own Story". Then he made the mistake of sending her to meet Mayor Frank Wansborough who promptly threw her out of his office.

Lots of laughter, lots of negative publicity.

Don Bondy

Don was a lawyer who became head of the Business Association. I think he thought he would subdue Jack Shanfield and get him into line. At board meetings Don would sling barbs at Jack whenever Jack stood to object, which was ALL THE TIME. Sometime Don's language was – to be kind – unsavoury.

Don was mercurial and we didn't always know what was going on. Politically, he was Conservative. One night he had everyone on the board called to leave word that he would be out of town but for each of us to go to such and such a place. When we got there – and weather-wise it was not a pleasant evening – we found it was a Liberal nomination meeting and he wanted us there to push for him to be the candidate. He didn't get the nomination and we left shaking our heads. What next?

From Don I learned, if there was an upcoming event, to 'flog the tickets.' Once we hired a small boat to take us out on the river for a special meeting and I did flog the tickets. Every one was sold. When we boarded, the skies opened up and we were drenched. Supper was delivered in cardboard boxes, which soon became soggy, and speakers could not be heard over the noise of the boat's engines. A lot of lessons were learned that night.

It was around this time that the Business Association became very concerned about something about to happen in the downtown and dispatched me to find out what was going on. It seems that Loblaws was closing its grocery store in the 700 block of Ouellette Avenue and, of all things, a BINGO PALACE was opening in that space. Horrors! You'd have thought it was the end of the world that such a nefarious outfit would be polluting our lovely downtown.

Little did we know then, what would descend on us: strip joints and massage parlours all over the place.

ART IN THE PARK

In 1971, The Art Gallery of Windsor volunteers were a big, active smart group of women who operated from the Gallery, which was then located in Willistead Manor in Walkerville. They had instituted Art In The Park the year before and it had been extremely successful but they couldn't find anyone within their ranks who could take it on again.

The Art Gallery Director Ken Saltmarche asked me to come and meet the volunteers, with the intent of taking over Art In The Park for a year. It was a warm evening and he had them seated in rows outside the open courtyard gates of the mansion. "Don't let them scare you," he whispered.

I give myself full credit for deciding we should expand the operation and take over Walkerville Collegiate for the Friday evening. My wonderful neighbour and friend, Renee Bondy, who could do anything, even while coping with a family of four, wrote a musical called, "We All Want", based on her four children who were always wanting something, and always four different things. It was to be an Art in the Park fund raiser.

We scoured the neighbourhood for actors and some of the cast included Katie MacDonald, Rosalie Bertoia, Renée and Duane Bondy, Ed Nead, Suzanne Bondy, and a great number of young people including my son Mark as well as several DeMarcos.

A male lead could not be found so my husband valiantly filled in. We sold all the seats and the audience liked it but for some reason the Windsor Star chose to review it as though it was a Broadway opening. The reporter did not like it and spelled out his thoughts in great detail, which miffed me.

On the Sunday afternoon, we had a mini tornado tear through the park, toppling booths. The participants reduced paintings to half price. Despite the unexpected excitement, the event was a huge success.

Needless to say, the ladies didn't scare me. In fact, I am still a volunteer. After the second Art in the Park was concluded, Windsor Art Gallery Director Ken Saltmarche said something like, "Now the potters in particular have nowhere to sell their products. Can you do something?"

POTTERY, PLACE RIVIERE & PERSUASION

After explaining to the lawyer Don Bondy about this problem he told me, "Take the BA Hotel". He owned this derelict historic building – the British American Hotel, which stood on the northeast corner of Riverside Drive at Ouellette Avenue.

I mulled this over for a few days and then called my friend Fran Odell who knew the downtown well. Before you knew it we were in business with a place we called "The Bazaar." We set our own hours and took in arts and crafts on a consignment basis. We knew from the beginning that we would never get rich but we enjoyed the people.

However, the empty hotel could be scary. There was not another soul in it besides Fran and me. In the winter a bitter cold wind swept down the river and attacked that corner. I dreaded going down to the bathroom in the basement at the bottom of dark rickety wooden stairs, and illuminated by just a single bulb hanging from the ceiling.

Fran was braver than me. Customers would ask questions like, "Are there rats in here?" This made me crazy as I could imagine such a thing but Fran didn't seem bothered in the least.

We were everlastingly grateful to Joan Hatch whose husband was President of Hiram Walker & Sons. She patronized us from the beginning since we did feature the work of excellent local potters.

While we were getting used to the business, Betty Behune stopped by with a proposition. Her father was going to build a kind of plaza in the next block over – the Norwich Block. She was setting up the shops there and she wanted us to be part of it.

So the delightful Place Riviere was built and we were indeed part of it and I can say again that it was a happy time. The concept was different and people were drawn to it as well as to the delightful restaurant, The Cheshire Cat. There is nothing like it in Windsor even today. Barney and Laura Boughner shared our space and sold china and wonderful coloured stemware.

Later, they made use of their red goblets when they opened the Green Man Restaurant on Ouellette at Elliott. At that time the restaurant had an enormous front lawn and the entire time they were in business they attempted to get permission from the City of Windsor to open an outdoor cafe. Unfortunately, they were blocked by red tape at every turn.

One day, businessman Elton Plant came in to talk to me. He had been heading a loosely knit association, which represented the downtown merchants, although not all merchants belonged. He said his family had just bought Lewis's Flowers on Ouellette Avenue south of Wyandotte Street and he wanted to lend a hand to his son who would be running it. He thought I should consider taking on his job as head of the Downtown Business Association.

Without too much persuasion I agreed and Fran went on to head up the Ottawa Street Merchants Association. I knew going into this new role that sometimes there would be almost no salary but I can say, even knowing about the finances and recalcitrant store owners, it was one of the best times of my Windsor life.

And so I seemed to lurch from one thing to another not seeking work, but something was always there waiting: managing the Windsor Symphony, running for parliament – it makes my head spin just thinking back.

It is only in the past few years that I realized that not all people were born with my energy and drive. Thinking back to a conversation with my doctor at the time, Tim Barnby, I have to smile. We were chatting about this and that and I said, "You know I seem to be slowing down."

"Les will be happy about that." he replied.

IT'S ALL POLITICS

Not too long after our return to Windsor from Oakville, Ontario in the 1960s, the Prince Edward Hotel went up for sale. It was a grand old edifice on a perfect location in the heart of downtown – the northeast corner of Ouellette Avenue at Park Street. I had toured the refurbished King Edward in Toronto and knew first hand what could be done if one only had the will.

As our family drove up Ouellette one day, the shuttered building grabbed my attention. Evidently, the Prince Edward could be purchased for just taxes.

"Do you mind driving over to City Hall?" I asked my husband.

He wheeled around and drove a couple of blocks over to the building. I got right in to see Mayor Wansborough. I explained to him what I thought should be done with this treasure, that the city should get involved and try and broker a deal to keep the building intact and then have it refurbished.

When I realized that my plea was falling on deaf ears I considered what mad thing I could do to grab his attention. Before I had a chance, the mayor shouted harshly, "The City of Windsor is not in the real estate business!"

I turned and left muttering, "If the City of Windsor is not in the real estate business, then who is?"

A short time later, the beautiful building was torn down.

THE HONOURABLE GEORGE DREW

I almost called him Gorgeous George but remembered that was what we called the Honourable George Hees. At one time we seemed to have a lot of good-looking dynamic men coming in from Progressive Conservative Headquarters. Not that it did any good with the voters but we enjoyed meeting them.

When I was young and head of the local YPC organization (Young Progressive Conservatives) the very handsome Hon. George Drew, our former premier and head of the Conservative Party of Canada, came to town. We organized a dance at the Lakewood Golf Club and sold tickets to everyone – Liberals and whoever else. The place was packed.

When I danced with our guest of honour he whispered in my ear the entire time. After the music ended my friends asked, "What was that all about?" I let them stew for a few minutes before giving them an answer. "It was all so romantic! He wanted to make sure that we knew we must field a candidate in the coming election. No seat must go uncontested."

When they had trouble finding a candidate, the hierarchy chose a really delightful and smart lawyer – Al Kennedy. Al was the brother in law of our good friends, Charlie and Claire Green.

As he was a token candidate the only effort required on his part was to ride about town in a convertible now and then, waving to people, accompanied by a car or two honking horns. We were alerted to where he might be riding and I remember my husband and I walking over to Wyandotte Street, waving and cheering as he drove by.

After the election, which the PCs lost here (no surprise), Al became head of the Ontario Municipal Board. He was made for the job. It was a perfect fit.

Some years later we were at a wedding reception at Essex Golf Cub and he was making a speech when someone called out "Will you come back to Windsor when you retire?"

"Sure I will," he replied. "I'm coming back to help Barbara run Old Walkerville."

Everyone laughed.

DIRTY POLITICS: MY TURN TO RUN

In the early 1970s I decided to run for provincial parliament. Towards the end of the campaign, Mrs. Cameron Montrose phoned and asked me to come to her house for a chat. She was a wonderful woman and had been an outstanding city councillor and had also stood for parliament. I was extremely fond of her.

She was in the neighbourhood so I could walk. It was a steamy hot day. I arrived to discover Mrs. Montrose, who was in her 80s, baking apple pies for a son who was coming for a visit; he loved her homemade apple pies.

Our conversation concerned the upcoming election. Or should I say, she talked and I listened. Mrs. Montrose explained that the local powerful biggies in the Conservative party could not vote for me. For the good of Windsor they must vote Liberal to stop the New Democratic Party. She felt I should be warned and not be too hurt at losing.

This was no grand edict from Toronto or Ottawa but something hatched locally. Why couldn't we have known this from the beginning? Well obviously they wouldn't get candidates if this were not common knowledge so it had to be a secret.

I was so naive.

I was to learn worse things about that election but I have chosen not to share this now in case lawyers (and there are always lawyers floating around a campaign) decide to sue. I am much too old to deal with that.

KNOWING

Many years ago my father's cousin Jean Putnam told me that every now and then one of us McKeens was gifted with extra sensory perception. She had a name for it – precognition, which meant that now and then that person could see ahead for a moment. It is not something that you can call up. I was sure glad to hear about this for I have at times been aware of something going to happen, generally not good, and wondered if anyone else did.

For example, one night towards dawn many years ago, I was downstairs in the living on the chesterfield. I had been reading and had finally fallen asleep. I half awakened to see a figure in white robes standing near me. It looked like all the pictures I had seen of Jesus and the figure made me know, without speaking, that someone was going to die and not to be afraid.

I assumed that it was going to be me and I was very calm with the news since I felt it was Jesus assuring me that all would be fine. When Les came downstairs that morning I told him what had happened and that I was going to die and he said, "Yeees, Barbara," and rolled his eyes.

But I had the wrong person. A few weeks later we got word that Les had the worst kind of cancer – stomach cancer growing in the oesophagus – and that he did not have long to live.

Les and I were part of a group of eight couples that met monthly for dinner and bridge, which included our friends, the Fullers and the Greens. We were also fortunate enough to also be part of a gourmet dinner group, and after dinners, we would play 21. On occasion, as a group, we went to Vegas to try our luck.

That spring Reg Miller had died, then shortly after that Charlie Green died, and then my husband was in London waiting to die. Les had a breathing tube attached to his throat and to communicate he used a pencil and a big writing pad. One day when I came into the room he held up a sign he had made which said 'GET OUT OF BRIDGE CLUB, BARB.'

We were only in our fifties and dying.

I am glad to say that those friends are still alive and well.

I don't generally reveal the mystical occurrences that happen to me to friends but one evening, many years later, I talking to my niece Babs Brown Holdsworth (on the Kersey side) who told me of an experience her mother had.

Many years ago, my husband's sister Dora had been walking down the street in Hamilton Beach when her grandmother, who had been living with them, passed her without speaking. Dora hurried into the house and said to her mother, "Grannie just passed me and didn't speak to me." Her mother looked and her and said, "Your grandmother just died."

It wasn't exactly like what I experience now and then but there seems to be a definite connection to the supernatural in our family.

Many years later as I was writing this book, it happened again. I started hearing the old hymn, "...softly and tenderly Jesus is calling, calling to you and to me." At first it was pleasant but when it refused to go away I got apprehensive. It was like a CD inside of me that I could not turn off. I eventually got used to it and took it as a message that I would die.

But I didn't die; my brother Ian did.

ALWAYS THE MUSIC (AND THEN SOME)

From day one we had a piano and music in the home. Les played and had a good-sized collection of classical records. I sometimes saw him listening with tears in his eyes. The music so moved him.

Meanwhile, the children all became rock and rollers.

In his later years, some of the residents at Central Park Lodge complained about Les' brother Ken bursting into song at the dinner table. On Guy Fawkes Day he would call a number of friends and without preamble recite "Remember, Remember the Fifth of November" in its entirety and then hang up.

I see this gift of music, painting and drama in the next generation and the next. They are all musically inclined and many of the boys and men are also good at woodworking, without ever having a lesson.

So when I became a Kersey, albeit with no talent, I blended into what is now a large lively family and I love them all. My son Mark plays piano and, like his father, can sing and play any instrument. At the moment Mark's daughter Emily, who graduated from University last spring, is off finding herself musically.

Musicians and artists in the next generation include my great nephew Jeff Brown who is Master of Music at the Lester Pearson School of the Arts in London. His son Scott has just graduated from the University of Western in Music and Business and his other son, Mathew, is in Halifax studying Graphic Design.

My great great nephew Jay Holdsworth is in a band and hopes to go to Montreal to advance in music.

My own family had considerable artistic and theatric ability. My father cartooned, his brother Frank Macdonald of Dartmouth, took up painting after retirement but it was Mrs. Beatrice Kersey (née Porter)'s brother who had real talent. In about 1900, when Beatrice was working as a mid-wife, her brother would correspond with her in a most unusual way. He would not include an address on the envelope, but drew a picture instead.

I am looking at one envelope now. There is a huge great home in the distance with a long, curving road leading to it. At the beginning of the road is a man with a pushcart on which are several boxes. On the side of a box is written, "Miss B. Porter, Bonnington, Cannon Park, Edgeware. Nearby is a signpost giving the miles to London.

There is another card showing a long brick wall on which is printed BLACKHEATH PK. SE. In front is an unattended porter's cart bearing a trunk on which is written "Miss B. Porter, c/o Mrs. Beckett, Penrith, Blackheath." Her brother seems to have worked in India ink.

This same uncle performed in English Music Hall as a ventriloquist. Years later in Windsor, he scared my husband half to death when Les was a little boy. His family was living on Howard Avenue facing Purity Dairy. Les came home from Prince Edward School and was just inside the door when a voice called to him from, of all places, inside the piano bench.

In addition to music, The Detroit Tigers were an important part of both our families. I can see my husband, towards his end, edging the lawn, with a radio propped on the garden fence, catching a Tigers' game.

Les's father, Sydney Kersey, was a tall, handsome man with a good singing voice. He too loved the Tigers and when he had the ballgame on, either on radio or TV, he never turned it off, no matter who was visiting. I can still see him sitting in a chair by the window in a spotlessly clean undershirt. My husband would ask, "Dad, why don't you put a shirt on?" but this would never happen.

Whenever my husband or his brother asked him, "How are you Dad?" he would answer, "PUNK." Nothing else, just "PUNK," which was a Limey word for "awful". And when anything good happened and you told him about it, he always said something like, "Them that 'as gets."

I found that as a young woman, I had nothing to say to such a negative person, but I won't deny that it is through his generation that the music and woodworking were passed down. And thankfully, there are all his lovely descendants in West Sussex, England.

As I write this I am struck by the wealth of tall men in both families. All were over 6 ft., except my father who was 5'11". I was told that at the beginning of WWI he did stretching exercises to transfer to the Black Watch where one of the requirements was you had to be 6 ft. When the men of the Black Watch were mown down in their first battle, which I believe was on the Marne, he lost interest in stretching. His brothers Clyde and Frank were both over 6 ft.

AND NOW

If the Kerseys are full of music, I am full of stories. My friends must tire of me spouting off with a story for every occasion. When I turned 90 in the fall of 2010, I knew I must write some of these stories down, and quickly for there would not be much time left. The first half of the book just spilled out of me with no notes or anything to guide me except a phenomenal memory. I could add to this part forever.

Despite the troubles with my mother, I was born with a bright, sunny disposition and it has stood by me my whole life and helped me overcome adversity.

Les has been gone 32 years, being buried on our wedding anniversary, Oct. 4, 1981. I've been lonesome but I got on with my life. I play duplicate bridge twice a week, do my own shopping and lug it to my apartment, visit Dani Bobb Friday mornings for my hair and then do chores. I look forward to weekends when several of my friends arrange a movie and dinner.

With all the starvation and suffering in the world it may seem frivolous to talk of my few ailments, but, when people learn my age, I see that they are truly interested in how I've managed so well, so far.

The middle aged and older ask questions like: Do you have Diabetes? Do you have a bad heart? What medicine do you take?

As far as I know I do not have either ailment and my medicine consists of eye drops and a small dose of aspirin at bedtime.

I do have familiar tremor (not Parkinson's or nervousness), which my mother also had. Since none of her family had it then I suppose it is one more thing to blame on the Irish grandfather none of us ever knew. The cure is a drink or two but at 7 a.m. it is not an option for me. Later in the day? Sometimes.

Young people are fascinated that I have lived so long and am still here doing pretty much what I have always done. They ask about my skin, which some people claim is wonderful, and my optimistic outlook on life. These things are inherited but perhaps both can be achieved if one sets one's mind to it.

I do have Glaucoma but so far it hasn't given me any problems. Worst thing that has happened so far has been the fallen arches, which means no more of my beloved high heels. Every morning I stuff prosthetics into hated oxfords, lace them up, and stagger around. Then I put in a hearing aid and a tooth retainer to fill a space for implants, which I now know I will not bother with. Weather permitting, I walk several times a week, often with my friend Lorna Baldwin.

I am very blessed with friends. Loving women friends that without my life would be bleak indeed. And I am in a perfect place. Two years ago I got myself moved into a small one-bedroom apartment with good neighbours. One of my bridge partners says, "Barbara lives in a village."

And she's right, I absolutely do. If I were to need help, it is here.

And I read. I am a voracious reader. I can't sit down or go to bed without being sure a book is at hand.

I realize that I am always saying, "I loved such and such a city, or such and such a person." This is true. Some years ago, in Sydney, Australia, I was late catching up with our small group in a restaurant. I arrived laughing, threw out my arms and said, "I love it!" I meant the trip, the country, life – you name it.

Someone in the group said, "Barbara, you love everything!"

And that summed it up. I am a happy person!

I have been privileged to travel the world and when I return and see the Detroit skyline, which is just across the river from my city, my heart leaps with joy for I know I am home in Windsor.

As I come to the end and look back, I can truly say of my life, *"Was I ever lucky!"*

Made in the USA
Charleston, SC
28 October 2011